A LIFE
in the
DAY *of*
HEAVEN

A LIFE
in the
DAY *of*
HEAVEN

Treatment for God-Trauma
Dr. Monte Pries

XULON PRESS

Xulon Press
2301 Lucien Way #415
Maitland, FL 32751
407.339.4217
www.xulonpress.com

© 2019 by Dr. Monte Pries

All rights reserved solely by the author. The author guarantees all contents are original and do not infringe upon the legal rights of any other person or work. No part of this book may be reproduced in any form without the permission of the author. The views expressed in this book are not necessarily those of the publisher.

Unless otherwise indicated, Scripture quotations taken from the New American Standard Bible (NASB). Copyright © 1960, 1962, 1963, 1968, 1971, 1972, 1973, 1975, 1977, 1995 by The Lockman Foundation. Used by permission. All rights reserved.

Printed in the United States of America.

ISBN-13: 978-1-5456-6832-0

INTRODUCTION

This is a work of fiction. Every human character presented here is fictional, including me. I am merely setting the stage for a journey; one that I hope will benefit you.

In this story, my function is to be a conduit of sorts. My role is that I am a friend of the main character. One night, my friend showed up on my doorstep and asked me to hold on to something for him, something which he brought to me for safe keeping. He then handed me the pages which you are about to read.

For this story's sake, you should also know that my friend is also my pastor. He is someone who has given me spiritual guidance for most of my, now considerably lengthy, adult life. This is a man who I tremendously respect. The fact that he is my friend may imply bias, but I regard this story to be a good read… something worthy of your time.

My pastor friend made a big show of demanding that I not share this story he wrote with anyone else. Seeing that you are reading this, you can guess how good I am at following instructions. The truth is that I really suspect that he wanted me to put this story out into the world. He was too modest to ask directly. I also think that he knows me well enough to realize that I'm a lousy keeper of secrets, fully capable of breaking any vow of silence no matter how sincerely I make a promise in the moment.

My friend also asked me not to change any of what he has written, he asked me to keep his story fully intact. His request begs the question... why would he be concerned about me changing anything if he really thought that I would just keep this all to myself? I think you can see my reasoning here.

I didn't change any of the content. I actually believe what he has written is a spectacular tale: the story of a man in crisis. This is a man whose crisis leads him to beauty, and then watches that beauty achieve a miraculous work. This work will change him, literally, *forever*. I think this story is darn creative and not to be messed with. He also worked so hard on this story and I want to respect that. He spent days poring over old notes and journal entries, as well as listening endlessly to audio recordings made at the time these events occurred.

I did, however, alter some of the structure: the format. I wanted to do something which gives the pastor's story the best chance to be understood. There were some challenges to what he just dumped on my lap. You see, a main aspect of the story is a series of dreams—perhaps even *visions*—that my friend had. I found it a little tough to distinguish when he was dreaming and when he was awake. So, whenever the pastor character is dreaming, I formatted those scenes *in italics, just like this. I hope that the italics will offer enough contrast to be clear for you.*

There are also, a couple of occasions, when the person whom my friend sees in his dreams, will turn and talk directly to my friend during the dream. I will differentiate those sections of the story, when the dream traveler talks to the pastor, **by typing them in bold print, like this.**

I would be remiss if I didn't divulge (I love telling secrets) that my pastor believes these dreams to be an accurate depiction of Heaven. Heaven is a place near and dear to my heart, as well as his. I also think that regardless of what you believe Heaven to be, this reading will increase some of its wonder for you.

There are some forces at work in this book which might leave you a bit confused, no matter how much is clarified. There is just some inherent confusion whenever the supernatural mixes with the natural—or when the temporary is intersected by the forever. We, in the temporary, are so accustomed to this cramped suitcase of space and time that we can't be found guilty when we step into timelessness and find ourselves to be a bit confused by it. When true life opens a door and allows us a breath of timelessness, we can be a bit dazed by the experience. All that to say that there are times when the language of past and present tense sequence are mixed up in the pastor's telling of his dreams of Heaven. I think that he was struggling with how to express his experience of Heaven as something other, something beyond past or future. Eternity needs no past or future, there is only now.

I hope this helps. I'm trying to strike a balance here. Too much clarity sometimes comes at a price. Knowing all of the contents of "Chef's Surprise Noodle Lo Mein" served at your favorite strip mall restaurant could get in the way of the enjoyment of a delicious meal. I wouldn't want that to happen here.

I am grateful that some things in this heavenly tale remain unclear. I am grateful that my friend allows this work to be more art than science. Art is one refuge in our culture where loose ends are tolerated. Art allows for there to be both form and funk. I have done what my friend has done and let the funk, let the mystery, stand on its own without explanation or apology.

It is my hope for you, that through my instruction and perspective, you will find the right amount of clarity needed. Feel free to refer back to this introduction anytime that you think it will help.

My friend once described his story as one man's dance around the edges of the truly mundane and the magic of life. He said that, in a lifetime of living, he still wrestles with which is magic and which is mundane. He will say that he suspects that he gets it wrong more often than right. He is too self-effacing; he has never embraced his gifts. His story will tell you, for example, that his preaching style was flat and formal. Don't believe it; I was there for the sermons that he will talk about. He was dynamic. The truth thundered in my heart, lifting me to the heavenly realms. His style was worthy of his substance.

With that, I will leave you. You won't hear my voice until, perhaps, the very end. From this point forward, any narrative is strictly his.

CHAPTER ONE

My story is for all who have experienced loss… for those of us who've had love brutally ripped away. While I really don't have any intention for any of this writing to be read, I write as if there were an audience, because a part of me wants people to know. I also think that the writing could be cathartic for me.

My beloved wife, Sarah, has passed and I am lost. My heart and mind plays ping-pong, back and forth with this reality. My mind knows she is gone. I saw her lowered into the ground — I know that she has died. My heart, however, refuses to believe this; my heart is too connected with my still-living love for her, my heart demands that its own subjective truth be known. My heart slams the door on the irrefutable reality which my eyes see.

My grief is simultaneously shocking and familiar. It can't be true, and yet, I know that another part of me has been preparing for this loss from the moment that she and I first met. Somewhere in the back corners of my brain, I've been strategizing for this loss forever. Apparently forever is not long enough, I am still not prepared.

A LIFE in the DAY of HEAVEN

In the face of such loss, I do what I have always done. I compartmentalize my emotions; this is the one thing that has enabled me to keep my head above the constant wash of grief. I am not proud of this, but I'm not looking for style points here... only survival.

Ironically, it is the curse of locking things away which has also pointed me in the direction of a more effective path to healing. An emotional tool has found its way back to me. A tool which is friend of both my head and my heart, and it is priceless to me. A gift from my past has come to me like a Christmas present wrapped up, hidden away, but rediscovered years later.

It is a gift that was, in fact, literally boxed, wrapped up and hidden away. You see, I was packing up some items of Sarah's. (Okay, pretty much everything that she owned.) These were items which my heart forbade me to throw out. It is a big pile of stuff. Anyway, I was shoving things back into the dark recesses of our attic, when I literally stumbled over a box long forgotten. It was a box of sermon notes. Sermon notes are tools of my trade. My trade is the clergy, I am a pastor. I am hesitant to admit this, because I should be one most able to make friends with the horror of death, and yet I struggle with it all.

The box was labelled "Sermon Notes, Fall, 1979"—forty years ago now. I was not in a habit of keeping my notes, so as soon as I saw the box, I knew precisely what it was. These notes were written a time when I had a brush with the harsh window of short-lived fame and notoriety. It was also a time when I experienced my one exposure to what I would consider to be the truly miraculous.

The power of a miracle was not the reason that I had shoved this box into the darkest corner of the attic. No, this box was buried next to old sports trophies and high school yearbooks, because the contents of the box also told the story of my greatest failing.

Stored in the box were four cassette tapes (it was a long time ago), and a collection of letters and copious notes simply labeled "Meg." I also found three sermon outlines to three sermons, which I would describe as the most infamous sermons of my long and unremarkable career.

Reading again my sermon notes, I find no mention of Meg, but I knew that what I spoke of on those Sunday mornings had just as much to do with her as it did with me. I had kept her role a secret for all these years, partially out of professionalism, but mainly out of shame. My shame washed over me again just by briefly rummaging through this box of notes.

Shame was, however, only a part of the story to be told. Shame drew my attention, but I am remiss if my shame eclipses any of the beauty of my memories of that time. While Meg and I were the very human players in the drama, the real story is about God, and His gifts to us. The real story is about Heaven.

In the Fall of 1979, I was a pastor of little renowned, a condition which would stay with me for my entire career. My faith was genuine and real, my capacity to weave pictures and stories was reasonably well developed. However, I was not charismatic, nor a compelling speaker. I could not "fill a room" as it were. Therefore, my ceiling of popularity was not high, and most of the time, I was okay with that. I had the love of a truly good wife—Sarah, and the riches that only comes with the raising of children.

The raising of children fell primarily on Sarah; I was predictably and comfortably ensconced in the predetermined gender role of that era. So, forty years ago I found plenty of reason to pretty much live at the Church where I pastored. I spent most of my workday time plugging away at my sermon development. My spiritual mentor once told me that preparation for a sermon should equate of one hour of prep for every one minute of preaching. You do the math. I was very conscientious.

My sermons tended to be of the intellectual variety. It's not that I didn't have an emotional connection with God—I did and I do. It's just that my Church was near a large, prominent university, so my congregation was more of a scholastic type and so it was good business to appeal to their intellectual sensibilities. Full disclosure, I was more comfortable with ideas rather than emotions, so the intellectual flavor suited me just fine.

Given my time constraints, I found requests for pastoral counseling to be more of an interruption than an opportunity. So, when my administrative assistant told me that a member of the congregation, only referred to as "Meg," had requested time for some spiritual direction together, I was annoyed. It is amazing; all of these years later and I can still recall the emotions of the time spent with Meg.

I mentioned that time constraints were one reason that I did little pastoral counseling, but it was more than that. I was also reluctant to sit one on one, in private, with a stranger who might require me to give more emotional depth than I was capable of summoning up on demand.

The third and final reason was that there had been a scandal in a local Church—a horrible situation. A pastor had been accused of causing spiritual harm to a member of their church during one of these "counseling sessions." The actual accusation was that of spiritual incompetence, but given that most people only read headlines, the assumption was that there had to be something more sordid involved. To me, spiritual incompetence was a damming accusation, but people like the flash and flesh of a torrid affair. The community would never get the satisfaction of scandalous testimony; there was simply nothing like that involved to be said, the jackals would have to wait for the next time that vultures circled above.

Spiritual incompetence is not only lacking in curb appeal, it is also not so easily defined in human courts as say, adultery. The jury had been unable to come up with a conviction. However, for this pastor, all the damage had been done and he was quietly dismissed. These possibilities haunted me.

For these liability reasons, I had asked Meg for permission to audiotape our time together, something which she readily agreed to. This is how I came to have these tapes and notes, which now filled in the details my memory can't fully recall.

As the sessions began, I was clear with Meg that our sessions were to be from the practice of "spiritual direction." I preferred the term *spiritual direction,* because it seemed to require less personal involvement from me. It wasn't "counseling," which carries some promise of wisdom, it was just direction. I could give direction. I just wanted to manage expectations. I would direct her to the Bible, to spiritual practices and call it a day. I was aiming for low risk, moderate rewards, but apparently Meg didn't get that memo, something which became apparent from the get-go. Her expectations of me were uncomfortably high.

The first of my six meetings with Meg started with her giving a context of who she was. She described herself as a person of deep faith, well-practiced in our Christian ways. Her angst was that, in her spiritual development, in her hunger for God, she felt she was unable to attain the intimacy with Him that she desired. She felt that she and God were at an impasse, and, refreshingly, she knew that she was the cause of the blockage. I say refreshing because I find that so many are quick to blame others for their lack of spiritual vitality. I find blame of this kind to be especially off-putting because there is too much blame is directed towards me from my congregation. They say "the pastor's too boring, he talks too long, and I just don't get anything out of what is said". These are types of things that I hear anyway, and these reviews hurt me when they make it to my eyes or ears.

Meg was different, she owned her issue, she described her problem as a lack of trust. She said she knew that she was called to release herself to Him, but she could feel herself holding back, and because of this she believed that she was only currently feeling a small portion of the pleasure which He held waiting for her.

She knew that the call to fully trust God came to her both from the Scripture and His inviting Presence. The problem was that when she got to the point of the release of her will, a profound fear cut through her like a knife. Meg described the fear as being a force which hit her physically, like a stab in the back. She said that she feared Him for no good reason whatsoever.

I said, in an admittedly snarky voice, "Well, they say that the fear of God is the beginning of wisdom."

She snapped at me and said, "I know the reverent, awed, fear of God's purity and beauty. I'm not talking about that." Her expression was all but screaming at me, "You idiot!" Meg had an interesting style of communicating; at times she spoke like a Shakespearean actress, formal and poetic. Other times, she sounded like part of a longshore gang working the docks.

I just really didn't want to get involved in all of this. With staff changes, with budget pressures, with sermons to write, and with the pressure to perform each Sunday, I just didn't have the space in my schedule for her. Honestly, I had hoped just placate her. A few scriptures given, a little hearing of confessions, a little prayer time, and call it a day. Everything by the Book, but nothing given of myself.

I asked what she wanted to get out of our time together… it seemed like the proper question to ask. She said something about a feeling that she was "Too earthly-minded to be of much heavenly good." I said something in return, but I have no idea what. I really didn't know what she was talking about, so I just stared winging it left and right. I shared some platitudes that were just enough to pass the litmus of Christian credit-ability, but not too much to offer any promise of sustained enlightenment.

I could see by her eyes that she wanted more, she needed more and she confirmed this by saying, "No offense," (a phrase which always precludes criticism) "but I hope you have something more to give next time. This wasn't very helpful, I expect more from you. I'll call your office later to set up something for tomorrow."

For the first time, I snapped out of being just stuck in my head and came up with some real emotions; unfortunately, the emotion which showed up was rage. I didn't know too much about what Meg was looking for, but I knew enough to know that rage was not well thought of in most spiritual-direction circles. I was sure they had a chapter in their books speaking against it, but I could barely contain my disgust. I wanted to lash out at her—she had stung me with her critique and I didn't like it.

However, I held my tongue because it would have been a violation of both my conscience and my contract to refuse spiritual direction to her just because she had, correctly, called me on the carpet. I had nothing... I said nothing.

That night I had my first dream.

I call these experiences dreams but I only label them that because I am physically asleep. I guess that they could be described as visions just as easily. Whatever they were, wherever they came from, they are unlike any other experience that I ever had. I was never more asleep, I was never more awake.

I dreamed of a woman on her death bed. I hovered above her as an observer of this scene and the scenes which would follow. As I watched the scene play out, I could feel every thought and sensation going on inside her. I knew that this woman was very much connected to me and I was to her. Of course, I was well acquainted with the phrase, "The two became one flesh," but this was the first time that I had really felt it. I knew her. I felt that I *was* her.

As both participant and observer, as both male and female, you would think that I would have felt conflict and confusion. Actually, I had never felt such an integrated, full-life experience. I knew her past, and I would come to know her future.

Once, I'd heard a psychologist say that we never really dream about anyone else, we are really only dreaming from, or about, different parts of ourselves. Perhaps what was going on with me, in these dreams, was just a typical human experience— but perhaps a bit more exaggerated. For someone like myself, who really only wanted to fit in, to be liked, to be comfortable, I wanted nothing to do with the extraordinary.

In any case, I felt that I had simultaneously stepped into the life experience of another human being, as well as coming into a hands-on discovery of Heaven. This story is both equal parts hers and well as mine, but as much as I try through my memories and words, I don't feel like I can do it justice, and there is sadness in that. Her story is simple and complex, as well as rich and sensuous in detail. This is what I saw as best as I can express.

CHAPTER TWO

I saw a woman in a hospital bed, surrounded by family. I can watch, and intuitively know, the important aspects of her life. This is what I know about her. She has lived, by most accounts, an unremarkable life. Reasonably well respected, her life had been equal parts wisdom and folly, private triumphs and public failures. And now her body is shutting down, it's expiration date having been reached. She is dying.

The numbing relief of the medical opiates had been pulsating through her arm for several days. She was, with loved ones by her side, experiencing what I could only understand as being death. The opiates offered a welcome relief from the suffering she had been going through, but a rational part of her also knew that those meds attached to her body signaled to the world that all hope was lost. This was to be her final state of being before the stoppage of what she has known as her life.

The people around her now, her family and friends, could do little to console her, even if they knew of the fear she carried in her heart, mind, and soul. And then she passed. There was nothing startling about it, no white light, no trumpet sounds... I saw her just slip from one place to another like the sliding of paper under a closed door. She knew that she had passed. She still felt herself to be conscious the whole time. She was moving to a place that only God knew. She was afraid.

In this new place, she was afraid to make any movements of her own volition, afraid to breathe, afraid to open her eyes, afraid that the opening of her eyes would reveal only unending darkness. At last, she was able to feel calm enough to begin to assess where she was and how she was doing. She sensed light and warmth around her, so she summoned all her courage and opened her eyes. She was amazed at what she saw.

She was struck by a different quality of life in her and around her. This was a different place, but strangely familiar, as well. Apart from the absence of pain, she didn't feel much different than before she'd passed. She became overcome with emotion, afraid to feel hope, but was extraordinarily relieved that life still seemed to be pulsating through her.

Never had she felt such profound gratitude that her senses were intact. She could see, she could breathe, she could feel, she could hear. She started to actively acclimate herself to her new environment. She was in a large room with rounded glass windows, sitting on a living room floor in a large home. From her perspective, she suspected that her new home sat perched on the side of a mountain.

She suddenly bounced up on her feet to look outside through a window. She was taken aback as she realized that no glass separated inside from outside—there was only open space. While this lack of a barrier was disconcerting, she felt like she should be afraid, but found that she was not.

She ventured a look outside and her senses were met with vast landscape views so rich and pure that she was beset by something akin to vertigo. She had to look away. She could only sustain brief glances at the beauty before her; it was all so pristine, so vibrant. The purity of what's she was seeing was causing her to feel disoriented and off center. As a way to protect her senses from overload, she brought her attention back to the room to regain equilibrium.

DR. MONTE PRIES | Chapter Two

Wanting to find a comfort zone, she focused only on the inside of this home on the hill. At first glance, the room appeared empty and sparsely appointed. She appreciated the tranquility of the room's simplicity after the sensory assault of the world outside the window. She needed the calming reassurance of the room and felt permission to just accept the offered serenity.

She delighted in the simple single note of one clean color, one smooth texture. This ease of design gave her time to breathe, space to adapt. Eventually, after much time has passed she forms some thoughts about the room around her. It was the simplicity of the room which served to make it easy for the woman to draw her attention to something truly astounding there in her midst. A beautiful, flowing, tapestry hung before her, seemingly suspended in mid-air.

In her previous life, she would have described the tapestry as classical, something like looking into a medieval world of beauty. Woven in the design were castles and endless rolling hills. There were distant seas, and sacred places of faith and worship. Three lions, regal and commanding, stood peacefully on a greenish-blue hillside. There were angels above, in flight towards a heavenly sun. A man, with an aura of wisdom circling above his head, sat in a posture of contemplation next to a fast-running stream.

It all seemed ancient, or perhaps better said, timeless. The tapestry dominated her attention. It was exquisite and the word "priceless" also crossed her mind. The tapestry gave the room depth and dimension. The tapestry was the first object of life and color that she noticed, after her first attempt to take in the purity outside this dwelling on a cliff. She emotionally bonded with the tapestry like one, newly-born, bonds with the first object of comfort it sees.

Her life within the room was safe. She felt less certain of the outside. Just remembering the brightness, the clarity, the vibrancy of what she had seen, still slightly unsettled her. She found whenever there would be anything even hinting at discomfort, she could simply look to the texture, color, and beauty of the tapestry to find comfort there. She took comfort in that it only required her fixing her attention on the tapestry for even minor uneasiness to disappear. She gave herself permission to just let this whole process unfold at its own natural pace.

The deep, profound security was doing its work, having an effect on the woman. As time passed, and she continued to feel completely safe, a growing hunger began to take shape. She yearned to take in more of the outside world. She also wondered where exactly she was, and whether she would remain alone in this new place.

She first became aware of a breeze from outside when she noticed the tapestry swaying slightly. It was a gentle movement, but it affected her enough to orient her sense of feel and smell. Her senses became increasingly more acute, and with it, a fragrance filled her being. What she smelled was fresh and clean: a hint of sweet rain, soil, rosemary, and sage. A new thought occurred to her, "I am completely okay." The fact is that she has never felt better. A realization has been knocking of the door of her consciousness, a knowledge that she had been afraid to put words to. The thought comes to her so strongly that she can't help but allow the question to blossom in her heart… "Could this be heaven?"

Feeling no evidence of her prior pain and burden, she took further inventory of herself. Her relief continued to wash over her like a wave. She was fully awake, fully refreshed, fully alive. Contrasted with the numbing that she felt prior to her passing, her new skin fairly tingled with energy.

She sat, dwelling on these newly-dawning revelations, for seemingly forever. She continued to take stock of herself. Slowly beginning again to explore, she took delight in breathing in the fresh smells wafting in on a breeze. The air, like a tonic, made her brain crackle with vitality and insight. Delighted at her heighted awareness, her emerging capacities, she opened up more and more of her sensuous awareness, and continued to gaze only at the tapestry.

DR. MONTE PRIES | Chapter Two

Time passed and she began to think…to develop a curiosity about the tapestry. Her bond with it could be compared to the way that, for years, a child might only look at their mother as an object of comfort, protection, and supply. But then one day, the child began to see their mother more as an actual human being. The child might then become curious about the mother in a new way, curious about who the mother is and what makes her tick. This is the new way by which the woman begins to consider the tapestry.

She started to suspect that there could be much more going on with the tapestry than she could first comprehend.

Again, it was her sense of smell which gently shook her out of her reverie. There was a scent in the air, like whiffs of licorice, and lavender on the breeze. The sweet, stringent smell acted to awaken her further and cause her eyes to look into the breeze.

Despite the height of the dwelling, standing on the edge of the precipice held no kind of trepidation for her now. As she looked out and about, a 180-degree panoramic view opened up. She continued to respond to the scents of licorice and lavender and moved to the far left side of the dwelling to locate the source of the soft breeze.

She looked up to a mountainside in the distance. It is thrilling to watch her absorb herself into this new space. As I watch her in my dream/vision state, I know that I am being vicariously altered by what she is going through. I know of secondary trauma, but I am learning of secondary pleasure through her.

The scenery upon which she gazes is reminiscent of the high desert lands of Colorado and Idaho. This is a relatively sparse landscape of mesquite trees and sage brush, lending its fragrance to wild flowering herbs like rosemary and sage.

All was clear; the air was so clean that she could see far out past horizons, which would have blocked her sight in the past. Her eyes easily drifted further away and to her right. She was grateful that she could take all of the beauty before her without the disorientation like previously.

She moved her eyes from left to right and the landscape shifted accordingly. More of an alpine picture came into focus. She could easily see a lush pine forest, soaring mountains and green grasses. A great valley of green separated two mighty forests, with a river flowing down the middle, creating a riparian vastness.

She gazed forever on this sight and this settled her in body, spirit, and soul. The river, which she could see in surprising detail, flowed for miles and miles. There were deep green pools of coolness gently flowing through the massive valley far away. Her sight followed the river as it cascaded over a cliff, spilling out as a powerful, surging waterfall, only to be picked up again, gently meandering through grassy meadows.

She understood something about the water's journey. She saw that the water seemed to be in the process of transformation as it spilled over another cliff, just up the valley from her home. Something about the power of the falls and the clarity of the air seemed to alter the water into something lighter, more effervescent, more alive somehow. As the water tumbled and fell through the valley below him, it rose like a living mist brought alive to her... something fresh, alive, and intoxicating. She continued to watch the water as it came to rest into the embrace of bright blue sea. A wisp of laughter lingered as a message to her, a promise of merriment to come, a gift that the river left in its wake.

Eventually, she came back into the dwelling and took her attention away from the spectacular show outside. She sat before the tapestry and she just breathed. She closed her eyes and thought of all the beauty around her and suffered the risk of a satisfied smile. She was safe; she knew that now beyond any and all doubt. There was no threat here, whatsoever—no pain, no suffering, no conflict. She soaked in this understanding.

She brought her attention back to the tapestry for no other reason than the joy it gave her. Again, she noticed that the tapestry was worn just enough, just enough toned down in its life and color and vibrancy, to be easily digestible to her senses. She stared forever at its beauty and was surprised to catch, out of the corner of her right eye, what appeared to be motion emanating from the medieval scene of lions and castles, and angels. She began to see that the water in the stream by which the wise man stood, was actually flowing; it moved down the length of the tapestry and flowed towards the edge.

The three lions were also on the move, they bounded down the hillside of the tapestry. The woman was enthralled by this, and she even thought that she could hear the faint rumble of a lion's roar. The living tapestry intrigued her to no end, but she continued to be in a state of curiosity rather than reaction of alarm.

Her curiosity was further piqued as she saw the water begin to flow off the woven work of art. The water moved straight off the bottom edge of the tapestry and right into a grotto of stone built into the floor of her home. She got up and walked cautiously towards the tapestry. The sweet fragrance of fresh waters drew her closer to the pool of what she believed must be a type of living water, a supernatural water. She couldn't believe it; the water seems so real, so she dipped her foot in.

She felt a strong, but pleasant tingle run up her spine. She slowly immersed herself into the sweet, soft water keeping her eyes always on the tapestry for comfort. She knew that the tapestry represented something very personal to her and she loved it. The dream traveler knew that she would wait for the tapestry to tell her its story. A story which, she was beginning to realize, will also become her story, her destiny.

Up until this point, the dream/vision was unfolding for me in a pretty linear way. But dreams seldom stay that way for long. The dream shifted, the woman stopped and looked me right in the eye and spoke. During the whole time that she spoke to me in the dream, I wanted to converse with her, but something forbade me. I wanted to talk to her, if for no other reason than to just get my own sense of self and some semblance of balance, but I couldn't.

When I remembered the dream later, I was struck again by the incongruences of what seemed to be profound shifts in her personality. It was like all of who she had been and all of who she was to become was present to see. I had been watching her in the dream, and all was kind and gentle, and compared to the initial panic of her death bed, she had been completely transformed. I couldn't help but see her softness and sweetness emerge in the presence of such beauty.

But then as she looked me in the eyes, I couldn't shake a strong masculine presence, a rough and tumble type personality. I was surprised at her edgy style; it was such a contrast to all of the soft and sweet that I had been watching. Regardless of how brusque and blunt she was to prove herself to be towards me at times, there would be no denying that she was generous in her desire to give. There also was no doubt that she had something to say.

Not able myself to speak, not able to make sense of any of this at all, I remained at her mercy as she launched into a long, one-way conversation, this is what she said: **"I know that this must seem weird, that I, a character in a dream, would be talking to you, the dreamer of said dream, but hey, welcome to my world, weird has become the new normal."**

I'm going to talk to you, I will dumb it all down some, but you still won't understand. How can you? You can read all of your books about Heaven, but until you experience this, you can't really know any more than I could before I got here.

I have to tell you, you have no idea what this is all about, you think you do but you don't. You think you know my mind, you think you know what I've learned, but you don't. I know, I thought there was a time when I knew something too, but I didn't. There is reason why He says, 'Lean not on your own understanding.' Kind of humbling, don't ya think?

DR. MONTE PRIES | Chapter Two

I can't even remember what I didn't understand, but I do remember the feeling of the whole earth-life thing, and by feeling, I really mean, *fear*. I was so tired; weary of the strain of living, tired of moving, tired of breathing, tired of breaking. But being as tired as I was, I did not welcome death.

Death had long held fear over me, it was the dark mystery. I dreaded the thought of my death, I always did. Sometimes when I was young, like really young, I would lay awake at night and just realize that I was going to die, and I would bolt upright in my bed, covered with sweat. Sometimes I would just get up and run out into the night, pounding the streets with my running, trying to get away from the dread that lurked behind me and before me.

Then it was all happening. It had taken forever, and then it all happened so fast. Out of self-preservation, I had begun to believe in death the way that a child once believed in Santa Claus. Perhaps the fears of death were the irrational musings of a child. Maybe your first realization that death is a real thing hits you hard, but maybe it is something one grows out of in time. You still believe in your head that death is real, but you never believe that it will actually show up one day and look you in the eye. Then one day it was real, death came and I knew it had come for me, and any fears about death which I repressed came back with terrifying force

Everyone else seemed to know that I was dying before I did, or better said, they accepted it sooner than I did. They had the luxury of knowing that death wasn't coming for them. They thought they were devastated by the news, but they could prepare for a world without me, but I could not. They wanted to show me that they loved me, and I appreciated that, but what really could they do?

They just stood around my hospital room looking sad, but their sad faces only depressed me, because I knew that they knew that it was all over. I also knew that they knew they'd be staying here, safe and alive while I was to plunge into the darkness of what I did not know. That depressed me, too.

I was so tired, just worn out. But I was also mad. I didn't show my anger, because seeing that I was at death's door, I thought being mad about it would be seen as bad form. But still I kept thinking, *isn't someone going to do something, isn't someone going to change the channel to some television show that wasn't about me dying?* Wasn't dying only something that someone else does, like getting hit by lightning, you hear about it, you might even know someone who was hit by lightning, but not you... not now.

Then I was gone... swoosh, just gone. It was the darndest thing. I knew it was happening, I was scared, it was weird, but I almost felt like I had done it before. Swoosh... gone. Gone, but gone where, gone how? It was so weird. I was somewhere else, and I still felt tired, but in a different way.

Before I was taken from that hospital room and landed had here, I felt tired because there was too much weight, too much weight on my body, too much weight on my life. The pressure of death was like a vise grip. Too much weight on my very being... very heavy. But when first arriving here, I found that I was not tired from the weight, but tired from the lightness. I was empty, poured out, poured out from nothing to nothing.

The main thing is that I had survived, and I guess that if I had the energy, I would have been happy, but I was too tired, so I just laid there. I had no place to go, no one to see, so I laid there.

When I finally felt strong enough to open my eyes, I was amazed. I was disoriented, but so happy that I could see. It was weird—but from the very beginning, I felt a constant feeling of safety. The pervasive feeling of safety started to change me. I was something like a bottle that had been adrift at sea, but now washed up safe on an island in the middle of the ocean. I washed up safe, sound, and secure. I knew that I had been spared from the dark depths of my previous fears. I was safe, so I wanted to cling to this place. I was like a castaway, embracing the solid ground of a faraway island after months of being adrift. But I never really felt like a beaten down castaway washed ashore, I was beginning to feel strong, I was beginning to feel like strength personified.

A sudden euphoria overtook me, like I was invincible, so I jumped up and ran towards what I thought was a glass window looking outside, but it was just open space. Remember… you saw it all happening. Anyway, I thought that, in my invincibility that I could fly off the edge of the house I was in. The house was high off the ground, but that didn't freak me out, the colors of this world were what freaked me out.

The colors were surreal, like everything in my life had been black and white up to this point, but now I saw true colors. It was too much, I was spinning, I wasn't afraid, but I was overwhelmed. I had to lie down and close my eyes and, when I did occasionally open my eyes, I could look only at the white of the walls within the room. What a trip, huh?

But once I got my bearings, I felt totally safe. I just had to go slow with the adjustment of it all. I felt sorry for you though; this must feel like a data dump that even a bright guy like you can't figure out. You have the pressure of time, I don't, poor you.

You see once I got here, I was in no rush. I didn't need anything. I wasn't hungry or thirsty, cold or hot. I didn't need anything, I didn't need to go to the bathroom, I didn't need to dress up, or clean up, or throw up, or anything. I was happy just to sit, to think a little, to breathe a little, to look for a little while at the colors outside. Now in this world, it's not that I'm out of time; it's that time is out of me, in other words, there is no time. But somehow, there still is a process to it all and I am grateful for the ever unfolding expressions of beauty.

When I dipped into the water of the tapestry pool, I felt so light, weightless... no stress. But I also felt more solid than ever before. Like I said, I feel like I'm repeating myself, I felt strong, steady, perfectly fitting in. And then, stepping out of that pool was like suddenly having your ears pop when you didn't even know that they were plugged. All of this potential that had been there all along came to life. I always sensed abilities in me but I couldn't name them, couldn't see them, and now I could. If was like instantly and perfectly learning a foreign language.

I had no idea that I could ever feel this good. It seemed like my sense elements of taste, touch, sight, smell, and sound had been multiplied by some power within me that I couldn't even define, except to say: God.

I don't know if it was my voice in my head, or God's voice in my head, but the words 'Behold, I make all things new' just came out of me when I stepped out of that pool. Anyway, I could go on and on, but here is what I want you to know, my friend, from the depths of my soul I now realize that I am fully safe, I am fully awake, I am fully alive, and someday, you will be too.

The best part of being here, in this place of persistent, mind boggling, body-altering beauty is that I don't have to do anything to make it happen. I'm so relaxed with all of this now. I don't have to try to be altered by beauty, I just am. It's like when, in your world, you want to try to make your skin darker, you go out into the sun. You don't try to tan, you just put yourself in front of the sun's rays and there you go, it just happens.

By the way, here there are no harmful effects of the sun; it's just perfectly warm, glowing, and sweet. I don't even know if it's like the same earth sun that I used to know. I don't know, I guess it doesn't matter.

Pretty deep, huh? Anyway, I had no idea how afraid I was on earth, constantly afraid. In the same way that I put my socks on each morning of my earth-life, that was how I put my fear on every day. Wearing fear was mindless and automatic. I know that I am not the only one to have done this. It was so pervasive. I was soaked through and through with fear, pride, and worry.

Like an old t-shirt, sunk to the bottom of a swimming pool was how I was. I was soaked with fear on earth and then brought out of the water to dry out of fear here in this place. I came here, dripping with fear and I didn't even know it. I didn't understand how filled with fear I was, how soaked with it I was, until the beauty of God began to dry me out.

Please forgive me for bringing a sad reality to such a sweet party, but you need to consider the sobering truth that you don't realize how weighed down with fear and worry you are. Your body, mind, and soul is filled with fear, and this is an incredible weight. Fear weighs on you… like a kind of obesity of the soul, and you don't know heaviness of the chains you drag around until those chains are obliterated.

You might feel depressed by being told that things are worse than you realize, but a sick person won't take medicine unless they are convinced that they need curing… and trust me, you need curing. The good news is that you have a much higher ceiling of joy than you can imagine. Beauty, security, and timelessness are the medicine, and there is an unlimited supply once you cultivate it.

Life is hard where you are at. Life is hard and most people blame God for that. People are confused. People confuse their present day realities with life, they are not. Then they confuse God with the broken circumstances of life. The thought is that if life is broken, then so must be God and His promises that are broken. God is not broken. But we blame Him and fear Him too, you fear Him more than you realize.

The real fear, the actual distrust of God is the great crippling disease of your world. It's not your fault that you fear in this way. How do you love God when you believe that He is at fault for all of the pain that you deal with every day—all the tears and fears, traumas and dramas? Right? He's to blame, isn't He? He could make it all stop, couldn't He?

This fear of God, this blame of Him is all wrong, but I was just as guilty as anybody else. The hardships of life just gave me an excuse to dismiss Him. I protected myself against Him, I probably still do. He made me, He could end me. I was afraid of Him in ways that I didn't even realize, so I closed myself off to Him.

But I didn't know any better, you don't know any better, how can you know what you don't know? How can a baby fly an airplane, how can a teenager act in ways of wisdom. People, young in earth years, only acquire wisdom when their brains have grown and they have been flavored by the sufferings in life? How can you understand what I now know? How can you know the seasoning of bliss and beauty, until they have been generously sprinkled on your little head? You can't. So, the bad news is that life before *Life* is even tougher than you can possibly realize. The good news is that you can do things to alleviate some of your suffering.

When I was where you are, like I said before, I put on fear like I put on socks—mindlessly, automatically, and something that I felt I couldn't leave my house without first doing. You see, fear isn't just in you; it is you, or at least, a part of you. What is probably so hard for you to see is that you actually want fear in your life. At some deep level, birthed and nurtured down through the ages of time, you carry the conclusion that you need fear. Fear becomes something that is just a natural part of you, a necessary part that you believe you need in order to survive.

Life is always evolving; a species will keep whatever it deems necessary to keep for survival. Human beings wouldn't keep fear; cultivate fear, unless it was something which is seen to be necessary. As a species, human beings are far from stupid—they keep what they need to survive.

Fear is a survival technique. Fear is not wrong, it is just grossly misguided.

You harbor a reciprocating relationship with fear, you feed it, it watches out for you. Fear promises to protect, but it is actually the treatment which kills the patient. Respect fear. Respect yourself for coming up with fear as a solution, and quietly walk away from it, if you can. Be quiet about it, put yourself in front of beauty and let beauty slowly draw the fear away from you.

Fear exists because you don't know, *really know*, what I've come to realize... you don't experientially know the immortality of your being, and that in your forever, all is made right. Fear has been there for you, as a misguided guardian, to protect you from death, to protect you from harm and from evil, but death does not exist for you, and evil is there for only a short season. Fear makes sense if life ends, if the stoppage of earth-life was your end, then you should furiously grip life and avoid anything which is a threat to your physical, emotional demise, but in the reality of this eternity, fear is nonsense.

The lie tells you that the end of your body is the end of you. It is not. When you know that you survive, that you can't not survive and thrive, then you have moved from survival mode into the realm of the eternal. In the eternal, you have everything that you need to thrive, and fear is no longer a tempting morsel to constantly chew on .

The human species once knew its immortality, but that has been lost. Humans were stripped of uninterrupted physical immortality by God. Fear of God and distrust of immortality resulted. Instead of knowledge of the immortality of the soul, humans clutched to themselves the only part of them that they knew was still intact—the physical. Ironically, the physical part, our bodies, is the only part in our human existence that is not immortal, and it is a minor part at that.

It is the physical which will die... no wonder I was so afraid. All I knew myself to be was the specific physical form which housed me, and that housing would cease to exist. I was right to be terrified, given what I knew to be true. Of course, all of this is easy for me to see now, and it will be easy for you too, once you leave earth. So, you will get all of this someday, but I wonder if I can help you now? I hope so.

It is easy for you to be anxious about life as you know it. You are anxious because you confuse your body—with all of its drama and trauma—with who you *think* you are. Like I said before, but it bears repeating, our present physical form is actually such a small portion of whom human beings are, who you are. Our earth bodies are not immortal, they stay behind to be grounded into dust on that cursed planet, you can see that now can't you. It's confusing because it wasn't supposed to be this way; we were created to not suffer death, or deterioration of any kind. We are immortal.

But we lost much confidence in even the word *immortality* when we, as humans, lost the physical immortality that the first of our species started life with. We threw the baby out with the bath water. The knowledge of immortality was the baby; the physical immortality was the bath water. Humans might think, "Well if this body is going to die, then the rest of me is destined for death too, I'm just chucking the reality that I will live forever out the window, also." Wrong. When we lost our way of immortality, we created a recipe for empowering fear.

We became obsessed with creating, maintaining, extending, and saving the only part of ourselves that was not eternal, and the spiritual, the part that is truly everlasting became dormant. We became a slave to our senses. Only that which we could see, taste, hear, and touch did we believe to be real.

Our true strength has always lain in those things we think of as invisible and therefore are minimized and ignored. Things like faith, spirit, God and love. In our fear, we endeavored to fight life and death, and to fight them only on terms that we could understand. So, we fought the power of eternity with the tools of the temporal and finite. We brought a squirt gun to fight a nuclear war. We need to reverse that equation, what you need to do is to fight the temporary things, the circumstantial things, with the tools of immortality.

Practice seeing your worries for being the temporary, unnatural state of being that they are. Good or bad, look at circumstances of life. Just do your best. Look at all things, no matter how high or low, with your eternal eyes, practice the truth that "this too shall pass." Know that the truth of unending good is just on the other side of the veil and that this goodness is your destiny.

I wonder if you can understand, be open to anything that I am saying. I wonder if you can undo for yourself some of the harm that you have inherited. I guess I wouldn't be talking to you if I didn't think that it could help you, and you wouldn't be listening if you didn't think that I could help you.

We humans are such a strange mix of nobility and folly. We foolishly grip our prideful insistence that we are in charge, that we orchestrate life, and we simultaneously refuse to accept and delight in the lofty height of immortality. One possible reason why you reject claiming and exclaiming immortality, is that you fear that to do so would be to proclaim yourself divine. We are right to feel shame if we offend our Creator, but seeing your immortal adornment is not to say that you are God, it is to enjoy a priceless gift which He has given. You need to know, to picture… to step into immortality. With the visceral knowledge of immortality, you soften the blows of life where you currently are.

Knowledge of the eternal in you and around you can take the edges off of just about anything. By the way, if you struggle thinking about the "immortal you", just think "the forever you," they mean the same thing. Each day practice seeing your starting point in life, less about the day you came out from your mother's womb, and more imagine when you were called out of nothingness into being by God Himself. He called out by Him to live forever. In the same way, imagine yourself each day as not having an end point to your existence, but rather see the inevitable breakdown of the form that houses you and that which you call *death* as your ticket out of the small, cramped, lockbox called *time*.

Death is your ticket to, not to your final resting place, but to your final living place, eternity. Yes there is rest here, but rest to inspire and empower you towards exhilaration. Earth-life is weird, Heaven is not. In your earth-existence, with all of your human despair and distortion, you have literally been a fish out of water flopping around on dry land, gasping for something there which you will never find. Soon you will be returned to the endless sea, where you belong, to thrive, heal, and soar.

I want to get back to my journey, a journey I know that you are watching me make, but I wanted to share one more practice to consider. Find that one thing that helps you feel the presence of God. What is it that you do, which acts as a vehicle to drive you into His presence? What helps you find a sense of nearness with Him, an alignment with forever?

There are different practices, I will share several. Some people read sacred texts and the inspiration lifts their spirits, some people pray and meditate, some people do great works of kindness and courage, some people sink into the beauty of Creation, some people get lost and then found in the magic of song and singing His praise. What works for you? Do this thing intentionally and regularly. Be strategic. Establish a baseline; get to know the spiritual connection between cause and effects. Okay, we'll talk again soon. There is so much ahead, so much forever for both of us. Peace.

I woke up from all of this, slightly amazed, forever altered.

CHAPTER THREE

It is a little bit fuzzy looking back in time, but I can still see myself that morning after the first of the dreams. It helps that this was a day of my life unlike any other, the morning after that first miracle, a day that I'll never forget. When I woke up, I first thought I had a hangover, but I knew that I hadn't had anything to drink; I rarely did in those days. But there was a weight, an alteration of consciousness—a depth of being that was unfamiliar to me.

The hangover feeling stuck with me, but I was confused. My brain was giving mixed signals. A hangover would suggest a diminished consciousness, and yet my mind seemed to be clicking on all six cylinders. This heightened state of awareness was thrilling. I suppose that there are different types of hangovers and what made me think *hangover* was that this was a peculiar kind of detachment, which I couldn't shake and in this case, I didn't want to.

Even when I got to the church, I still couldn't shake off the effects of the dream; it was like I hadn't really woken up. Even the realization that I had agreed to see Meg that day was not enough to jostle me back to my everyday reality. I looked blankly at her name, written in my appointment book, "Meg." Meg? It took me some time to even realize who she was. I was in a heavenly hypnosis and it was a rude awakening to come back to this place of worry, fear, and pride. Then the realization of who Meg was all came rushing back. She was the dissatisfied congregant, the one who didn't think much of my spiritual skill set.

She came in, looking angry. She was acting in ways which were starting to scare me, and especially then when I was young and bullet proof, I had no time for that. So, I told her the dream just to keep her quiet, it seemed like my best defense. Telling the dream took up our entire time, something for which I was grateful. I didn't tell Meg the story because I thought that it might help her, or not even just to ward off the verbal punches which I suspected were coming. I told her the dream because it held me completely in its tender clutches. I told her the dream not because I valued her, but because she was a captive audience and I had to tell somebody.

I was amazed that I got the whole story out. I felt as if I total recall of every piece of the dream. I was blessed just in the re-telling, like I was reliving it more than remembering it. You know how many people say, "I don't remember my dreams." Well, I could not un-remember this dream. It was just like reading a teleprompter which the dream seemed to have implanted in my heart. Afterwards, Meg was quiet for a moment or two and then said, "Your counseling skills are pretty weak, don't they teach you in counseling class to listen more than talk?"

She was right. I said, "I guess I do more preaching than listening. Sorry, it's who I am. I'm a little rusty at what you seem to want from me."

"It's okay," Meg said. "You're a good story-teller. A lousy counselor, but a good story-teller. You were half hypnotized when you took up all my time, and I think I was too. Your dream actually helped me... a lot. Either you're more brilliant than

I thought you were, or you, my friend, had a vision from the great beyond. Anyway, thank you. I'll make another appointment for next week, you did reasonably well today."

I could have felt offended by her candor, but a bigger part of me was just happy that I had something useful to give her. I didn't have the inclination to untangle Meg's weird, conflicted way of showing gratitude, so I just let it pass. I was still feeling affected, but now it was more like the heady buzz from a good bottle of wine. Instead of feeling slightly cloudy, I felt a rare clarity which I had not felt prior, nor have I ever felt since. No fuzziness, only focus.

Writing from this energy, I came up with a full sermon in less than an hour. I wrestled with whether I would actually speak the words of the sermon which I had just written. I was confident that there was meaning in the words should I could choose to actually say them out loud. These might have even been words that I had been anointed to speak. They came from an unfamiliar place inside me, and there was, to me anyway, an alluring scent of inspiration about them. This whiff of an original idea or two created a conflict in me, inspiration implied the threat of real impact, and I was afraid of impact. I was afraid of being noticed, afraid of being taken seriously. I had worn mediocrity like a comfortable pair of jeans, not much to look at, but very familiar. Now what I was I to do?

I had always told myself, at some level of half-consciousness, that I could be great if I tried. But why look like I cared enough to make an obvious effort, why look like being taken seriously mattered to me? I told myself that I was too humble to be impactful, that the powerful pastors were ones who took themselves way too seriously. Success would lead to pride and, gosh darn it; I'm not just like all the rest who let success run amok, I'm better than that. Why should I give opportunity for pride to take hold? Later I would come to see, of course, that all of this was nonsense. My theory of me being better than other pastors by wearing mediocrity like a badge of honor was, of course, pride personified. I didn't know that then.

A LIFE in the DAY of HEAVEN

When the Sunday morning of what came to be known as, "The God-Trauma Sermons" came around, I still was hesitant to broach the words and feelings that the dream had inspired in me. When it was all said and done, I decided to move forward. When I read over my sermon notes, I liked the sound that some of these words made when strung together. I was always a sucker for a good lyric, the turn of a phrase. In other words, I was too vain for my words to not be heard. Eventually, I put all of these thoughts aside and I just went with it. I went with my first instincts which said that even though I didn't really understand what these dreams were about, or what they were inspiring in me, I could feel their depth and dimension.

I was full of insecurities and conflict, but I was also excited about these dreams on a whole variety of levels, some sincere, some self-centered. Maybe there was something here for me? Maybe I could sell the dream story to Hollywood; maybe I could land some big speaking gigs from it? Maybe there was fame and fortune at the end of this rainbow? I was bouncing between greed and neurotic insecurity—neither a good starting place for preaching.

When I gave the sermon, I couldn't help but being aware of where Meg was sitting. She was seated in the third row, left wing, tenth seat in. She just sat there. I don't know exactly what I expected, but, she gave nothing away of what she was thinking or feeling. Meg was non-committal in her facial expressions, conveying none of the positive responses that I wished for my words to inspire from her. I wanted her to be impressed, or at the very least, approving.

I was struck by two realities as my sermon plowed forward. One thought was that, despite the theory that men are thought to be especially poor multi-taskers, I found that I could preach my sermon while simultaneously tracking not just with Meg, but also with various other people in the congregation. I was testing the climate of the room constantly, looking for evidence of rejection, but I was pleased to see that the people seemed to be reasonably pleased with what I was putting out there.

My second realization was that as the sermon progressed, my need of Meg's approval was ramping up even higher. I couldn't stop looking in her direction. She just continued to sit there, stone faced, like she was purposely not giving me the satisfaction of me thinking that perhaps I had some spiritual depth after all. Her bit of half-hearted validation from the end of our last session was like the taste of a mind altering drug in my mouth. A drug which I began to crave.

I could also see that my attention towards her was causing a reaction from my wife. The fact that Sarah had noticed me looking Meg's way bothered me to no end. Sarah was sitting in the front row and was following my eyes, which kept wandering. I steeled myself to not look Meg's way from that point on, but it was eating me up inside. These are things that I remember from that day, what I don't remember is exactly what I said.

Below is a sample of what I probably spoke to the Hillsdale Congregational Church that Sunday. Below are the notes, the sermon outlines which were part of what I had found in the box in the attic. In my career as a preacher, I would always write out the main ideas, not to follow verbatim, but to keep a flow. A part of me wanted to practically memorize my notes, but I knew enough to give space for some spontaneity and life to flow. My belief was that people could tell what was real and what was canned and I wanted to keep things real.

Truth be told, I wanted to keep things real, but not too real. The sermon came out of the Genesis story of Adam and Eve, and some of the things I wrote in my notes were provocative. I am certain that I left a good part of this material out because of wanting to maintain a low profile. For example, I am sure that I never would have allowed myself to publically speculate on Adam and Eve's frame of mind, or their motives and methods. Who was I to raise questions and speculations? I had no authority. It was just my style to keep a "big bang" idea in my back pocket just in case I needed to wake my listeners up. I also found that if I wrote bold, even outlandish ideas in my notes, it was easier to soften them than to empower bland words and ideas with life.

Despite my doubts, I had obviously been impacted by the first Heaven dream, and I remember telling myself that I would have to watch myself, that it was dangerous to speak about the nature of things with the same kind of certainty that the dream traveler had spoken to me. I repeated the mantra that flying under the radar must remain my friend.

These notes are in pretty good shape, given how old they are. They have been well preserved through benign neglect. Augmented by my faulty memory, these notes outlined below are all that remains of the most important sermons of my life. They are organized by numbered thoughts and capitalized headings. Please know that these are speaking points of the ideas that I wanted to pull from. These notes are often fragments of thoughts; they are like rocks in a river, landing points as I venture out in faith. Also, as stepping stones go, they don't necessarily follow a concise, logical flow.

I put the different main points as headings that I could easily see from the pulpit. These were the points of emphasis which would guide me through the tenuous journey of preaching on this important Sunday morning.

#1 ADAM AND EVE IN US

We were brought out of nothingness by the loving, eternal, omnipotent God. We were formed in His image for His purpose and pleasure. Being formed in His image allowed us the capacity to be in harmony with Him, and His will. Harmony with Him, as the Creator of life, allows harmony with all that He has created.

I believe in the truth of the biblical account of the creation of humankind. For the purposes of this discussion, I will be using the description 'we' as it relates to what we have uniquely in common with the biblical characters, Adam and Eve. They are our ancestors; they were the first of our species, so the word 'we' includes the whole of our human species.

It was Adam and Eve who experienced life as God intended it to be. They experienced the full measure of the beauty of God and the life He created; they represent the best of the human experience.

As the originals, Adam and Eve's influence on us, as human beings, is without equal, save for that of Jesus Christ. Their seminal life experience echoes down through the very DNA of the whole of humanity to follow. They were the big bang point in the origin of our species. The elements of their lives exploded out from this beginning point, carrying with it their natures, their memories and their position in life. Their life experience was transmitted down to their offspring and continues to be passed on to this day. When they rebelled against God's one command, their state of grace was obliterated, and by extension, we, their descendants, lost our fully God-graced existence was as well.

It is a common theological construct to think of how, as the human origin point of sin, Adam and Eve bestowed on us the shadow of death and separation from God. It is less common to acknowledge the possibility of how Adam and Eve could have also given an inheritance of other vestiges of their life experience. Could it be that Adam and Eve also passed to us echoes of light and beauty, stature and something of the lofty standing consistent with their royal position in the Garden of Eden? Perhaps there are the great, unrealized potentials latent in all of us—potentials given by God, inherited through Adam and Eve, available to us if we wake up to them.

Could we have inherited the now forgotten memory of His beauty, and our oneness with the beauty of Him? Perhaps we as human beings have forgotten what Adam and Eve once took for granted; it seems that we have lost touch with their full pleasure of the blissful union that our ancestors once enjoyed with God. Is it possible to recapture some of that ancient splendor?

We have forgotten, lost sight, that we human beings were once so merged with God that this union defined all of human experience. Our task in life is to find oneness restored. We also know that Adam "knew" God and the word here was the same that Genesis uses when describing how Adam "knew" Eve. Adam and Eve were one, and they were one with Him. The words of Jesus also touch on this oneness. Jesus is the great redeemer and restorer of oneness. He is the bridge from what was there in the beginning to that which will be fully restored in Heaven. Borrowing from the imagery of Genesis, He described Himself as the bridegroom and that we are His bride, and how the bride and the bridegroom become one flesh. Jesus prayed, in another garden at another time, that His followers would be one with Him as He and the Father are one. I believe that we once lived out the type of oneness with God the oneness which Jesus prayed for us to know in His Priestly Prayer. This is the ecstasy, now forgotten, that God intended for us.

Consider the depths of Adam and Eve's shock as the ecstasy of their existence was obliterated. To their hearts, minds, and souls, rejection was impossible, expulsion unthinkable. Childlike trust doesn't begin to describe the security which they had in God. The depths of their being read like an open book, no fears, no defense.

So much or human experience echoes from the Garden given and the Garden lost. What ramifications came from the trauma of life snatched away? What else may we have inherited from Adam and Eve? Could something else sinister come to us as part of the package deal called original sin? Could there be other shadows to darken our spiritual doorways which also came from the Garden of Eden? We may have the joy of His original beautiful intent in the recesses of our hearts; and we believe that we carry the dark stain of sin as an inherited disease, but there may be also be an accompanying fear birthed at the cross point of the light and the dark.

Could the horror of utter abandonment send shock waves not just through the bones and blood of Adam and Eve but also the whole of our human species? Was complete trust in God here on earth also a casualty of Adam and Eve being thrown out of the Garden of Eden? Could we still carry, through no fault of our Creator, a condition which distances us from most fully trusting Him? A condition may exist, as a result of our species expulsion from the Garden, of what I call *God Trauma*.

#2 GOD TRAUMA

God trauma, like any trauma, would be a condition which requires treatment. Trauma is a deeply disturbing or distressing experience. It is often unexpected and uncontrollable. Trauma, untreated, would be also a condition which sadly has a long shelf-life. Sometimes the residue of trauma can last long after the person is removed from the traumatizing event.

Memories are imbedded, able to be triggered by other elements which existed in the vicinity of the trauma. Logically, these triggers would not be thought to carry any real threat, but by virtue of their proximity, they are now bound together with the actual source of the pain.

Certain sights, smells, tastes, or a sensation of touch, which are not in and of themselves horrifying, can be triggers. Certain triggers are able to elicit a fear reaction, similar to that which the true threat carries. For example, for battle combat vets, the *thrap thrap* sound of whirling helicopter blades carries almost as much fear as sounds of bullets whizzing by their heads, even though the helicopter blades are benign when compared to bullets.

The trauma, whether carried forward by memories or by associated triggers has a physical component. The trauma is thought to be *somatized*, meaning that its effects are felt in the body, that some aspect of the distressing experience is carried and stored in the body, not just in the mind. Therefore, the treatment of trauma often has a way of altering and relaxing both the body and the mind of the one suffering. It's like the brain has been shaken, the body distressed, and both need to be soothed to offset the effects.

#3 ADAM AND EVE'S DEVESTATING LOSS

Adam and Eve were in full harmony with God and life and each other. Their whole identity was created and immersed in their experience of oneness with God. They knew nothing of themselves independent of Him. Life was from Him, and the beauty pulsating in and around them was all about Him. They existed to enjoy Him and the gift of pure beauty which He gave them. They gravitated naturally towards Him; they orientated themselves to Him as non-reflectively as a flower traces the path of the sun across the sky. His life was in their blood; His voice was in their heart and mind. His dignity was in their steps, His song was sung from the depth of their being, His supply was constantly extended towards them. Traces of this life reverberate also into the forgotten depths of our being.

With the sin of Adam and Eve, the bond was broken. They went from a golden, indestructible cord of unspeakable strength, power, and beauty to, by comparison, a fragile thread. The voice of God, the voice of thunder, the voice of a thousand mighty waters was now still and small.

When they broke from Him, their life was shattered. All of what they knew to be true was ripped from their very being, and they teetered on the brink of physical, psychic, and spiritual annihilation. This was their God trauma, and by extension, our God trauma as well. Their experience, so bone-chillingly real to them, was passed down to us as a shadowed, shared memory.

Of course, this trauma suffered at the hand of God was not in any way His fault, or His purpose. As perfectly holy, right and true, He was fulfilling the promise of His pure Word spoken to Adam and Eve. He is eternally blameless and loving. He is the perfect Father, and it was the rebellion of Adam and Eve that brought devastating consequences to bear on their own lives. And yet, as the consequences were ones measured out by God's own hand, trauma was now linked to Him and His ways. God's hands, forever right and pure, were now instruments associated with heartbreak and His people shrunk away from His Presence.

Banished from their garden, stained by the disease of sin, distant from their Source and Supply, Adam and Eve were lost, afraid, and traumatized. They were shadows of the regal beings they once were. Their life of order, purpose, and bliss was nothing but a haunting memory. How bleak all must have looked, like shifting from multi dimensions of color and vibrancy to a (by comparison) flattened grey shadow land.

The magnitude of their shock still reverberates in the whole of human existence. So much dignity and capacity lost through the intervention of God, and then even more spiritual, emotional capacities were lost as physical survival shot to the top of the food chain of priority and pushed the spiritual aside.

#4 ADAM AND EVE'S DIMINISHED CAPACITY

They were cursed from that day forward with a life of sweat and death, to suffer pain and the ravages of decay and time. They were called to face challenges which their life had not prepared them for. They must have felt that their new life experience was like facing a mighty army of trials and tribulations without any of the weapons necessary for survival. They were broken people in a broken world, suddenly at risk from a thousand points of threat.

They were at a true crossroads. They could have taken responsibility for their choice and humbled themselves. Banished from the garden, the wounding would still have been devastating, but it would not have been poisonous. The toxicity came from the choice to hide from their responsibility, and their simple, blessed character was permanently compromised for the duration of their earth-life experience.

They gave into pride, they gave into fear. Perhaps their fear told them that feeling the full weight of responsibility for all that they had lost through their actions could have been utterly cataclysmic. Perhaps their pride told them that confession would trigger an unending shame and the risk of vulnerability to a potentially punishing God.

Adam and Eve were, evidently, and for good reasons, novices at taking responsibility for their mistakes. Pride and fear perhaps whispered in their ears something like, "God practically destroyed you when you were strong, do you really want to reveal any fault before Him now that you are so weak?" This original refusal to find humility guaranteed that Adam and Eve would be defined by the trauma of their lost paradise.

Persuaded by fear and pride, Adam and Eve began to build a barrier towards God further distancing them from relationship. The pathway of humility has always been the door which God has used to transport us into His Presence, and now humility began to be seen as weakness.

This refusal to confess became ground zero for all of the internal conflict and duplicity to come not only for Adam and Eve, but for the whole of the human species that came from their seed. How easily have all of the descendants of Adam and Eve walked the well-worn path of pride and self-deception. The saying that, "It's the cover-up, not the crime which will get you" can, perhaps, trace its origin to this singular point in history.

They knew that they still needed God, but in this barren existence brought about by this altering event, they needed someone to blame. As they eliminated themselves as responsible beings (although the guilt could never be fully shaken), they looked again at God. The memory of Him as their Source was still in their hearts, but instead of the Source of only good, and light, and love, He was now also the Source of their sorrow, sadness, and suffering. Adam and Eve became the first to confuse God with the brokenness of their own self-inflicted pain.

They hurt, they were terrified. They found a name for their pain, and that name was God.

#5 SURVIVORIAL MECHANISMS

Not willing to risk the anguish of their responsibility, they shut themselves down even further, closed their hearts even further to Him. Major remnants of God's gifts of goodness and His capacity were deadened with a generalized shutdown of their true beauty, their true depth and dimension. They made a choice to cloud their sight and dim their ears, out of fear that they might not survive the seeing and hearing of the truth.

To repress their awareness cost them some of the exalted capacity they once possessed. To lose the memory of God's purity, goodness, and beauty was a terrible price to pay, but to be constantly mindful of the memory was a pain that perhaps they could not bear. Deaden knowledge, deflect responsibility, deny the loss—these are time-honored human protections that were likely birthed as Adam and Eve hid their nakedness. If God's Holy Name was diminished in some fashion in the world that was, and the world to come, so be it, at least Adam and Eve would still survive the devastation, these kind of rationalizations took center stage. I wonder if this was their mindset. I would also confess that in the wake of the kind of devastation they felt, I would be tempted to think of myself first as well. Not knowing life without the sin nature inherited, I still can't help but buy wonder if I would I have handled their circumstances anything better than Adam and Eve did? Would you?

God brought onto Adam and Eve a curse and introduced a new order of life. Their new life involved a scratching out an existence type of living, a pain-filled future with the horrific prospect of death waiting at the end of the road.

Cast from the womb of the garden, distanced from God, both by fear and by consequence, their resulting God-trauma panic caused them to shift from a thriving life to a survival-based life. Survivors think and move through life differently than ones who thrive. A survivor's vision narrows. They see only the immediate, and they look primarily for that which will increase their chance to survive. They don't feel that they have the luxury of artfully navigating the seas of life, instead they look to find any random debris floating by and death grip that flotsam, willing to go anywhere it takes them.

When people are adrift, they feel that they are at the mercy of the elements; they cling to anything which would take them out of the helplessness they feel. Adam and Eve would be craving the power which once grounded them in security. In the face of such powerlessness, they desperately craved for any fragment of what once had been theirs. They still had portions of connection with God, but, compared to the original oneness, it was a distant connection, and a relationship defined more by memory than intimacy.

In the face of such distance good and present suffering, they had generalized and externalized their personal trauma and felt God now was someone not to trust. They could reclaim some of their former dignity, but they would need to take the pathway of humility and responsibility.

For Adam and Eve and their descendants, humility and responsibility were treated like two great and powerful ogres living under the bridge of a path greatly feared. How could they humble themselves and take this path, how could they submit to the One who they felt had utterly forsaken and abandoned them? Instead of pushing through their fear with the power of submission, they searched within themselves for vestiges of power separate from God. They needed something, anything, and they needed it fast. Pride was a quick and easy compromise.

#6 FREE WILL AND GOD GIVEN PRIDE

God had given Adam and Eve the blessing of free will. They had personal autonomy even if it was not something which they were conscious of. This free will carried with it certain elements of personal power and pride and responsibility. Adam and Eve were caretakers of the garden, empowered to act in ways which reflected their personal choices.

As in all successful endeavors, there would have been personal pride in their part in the ordering of this perfectly harmonious place. The dignity that comes from hard work and accomplishment, the pride which is birthed in successful choices would have given some unique flavor to their life experience. The whole of their being and identity was immersed in God as their source and supply. Their personal power, responsibility and pride would have been watered down by the sheer strength of their love for God. Original pride, in the context of Adam and Eve's all consuming union with God, was blended purposely as a useful state of being, like a shot of whiskey swimming in twenty-gallon vat of water. Pride offered up a little flavoring, but not much more. There was a little kick of personal pride, but any chance of toxic effect was more than offset by the purity, innocence, and childlike awe of their Father /Creator / Supplier of Beauty and Bounty.

#7 THE EMPOWERING OF PRIDE

But post garden, they craved any vestiges of power carried over. They had lost their awe, their innocence, their trust, their identification in God's family as the noble prince and princess. The deep reservoir of purity, humility, worship, wisdom, and joy had leaked away—like liquid in a bucket, riddled with holes. What did remain was their identity separate from God. God, in the garden, was their ever-expending, ever-deepening symphony of sight, sound, beauty, and supply. They came away from the garden, not as treasured instruments in a symphony of power, but as a single solitary note still echoing from within. Their graceful God-given power was gone, their personal power and pride remained.

Ending prayer.

There you have it. These seven points above provided the sermon outline from which I preached after first meeting Meg. Of course, all of this would have been a lot to digest in one Sunday morning. Like I said earlier, I know that I didn't get to all of these points on my outline; I probably touched on half which I wrote out here, but a lot of thoughts were swirling in my head and heart.

The swirl of thoughts and feelings would do nothing but intensified in the days ahead, and I would begin a less than titillating tussle within my heart which ended up engaging the whole of my being. Heaven had given me a dream, but perhaps something else had given me Meg. I just didn't know where she fit in. Heaven had inspired a sermon, but I had no idea what Meg would inspire, but looking back now, I can see that her impact on me was just starting to be felt.

CHAPTER FOUR

Reading my sermon notes now, as you have just done, I'm struck at how stiff and formal they seem. I am pleased and touched by my thought that there is true inspiration here, but I wish that I could have infused these thoughts with a little more flavor, a little more spirit. I always thought of myself, while not a dynamic speaker, at least a genuine one, someone with warmth. I would like to see myself as that way, but I don't know… maybe just wishful thinking. I don't see much personality here in these notes and I doubt that I had reached the spoken passion which the words deserved.

It was the fear of hearing the flatness of my voice which caused me to not keep the recordings of any of my sermons. I hated the way that I sounded, so any recordings of old sermons would have been the first things to get tossed. I listened to one of my sermons once and it practically destroyed me. It took about a month to recover from the shock of what I was hearing on tape was so different that I had imagined myself sounding from the pulpit. I was just so rigid then, frozen and anxious to please. I doubt that I allowed anything free flowing, but I guess that doesn't matter now.

A LIFE in the DAY of HEAVEN

In addition to being surprised by such a formal writing style, I am also struck by the content here. I honestly had never really thought about Adam and Eve, their issues, their loss, their struggle prior to my dreams, and my interest in them left as quickly as it came. I read my notes now about Adam and Eve and how their fall from grace impacted the entire human race. Even though I had authored these thoughts, I am still left with a thousand questions.

Some of the ideas that I had written seem so full of curiosity and speculative possibilities. I wonder why I never followed up with these fragments of inquiry with more concentrated study. Also, why were none of these thoughts truly sustained in my personal life? There were practices and perspectives that could have been relevant to my Christian growth and development, so why did I bury all of this? I read these notes now and am surprised that I even wrote them. I don't recall thinking about any of this in depth. These thoughts were like the dreams, they came and they passed.

The only sprinkle of style that I can see in my sermon notes are, as I mentioned before, is my love of words and ideas. I was fascinated with the theological and theoretical underpinnings of life back then. The down side of purely theological preaching is that words apart from feelings can trap you in your head. The mind often lacks the heat of emotional spice necessary to engage the palate of the heart, so I imagine that many in my congregation were accustomed to going home not spiritually fed. This makes me sad as well.

But now, as time and life color me more grey than black and white, my heart awakens and feels the space to feel sadness long denied. I can now get choked up by things which I would have raced by when I was a younger man. For example, looking at my sermon notes, I can't help but tear up while reading the Adam and Eve story.

The more that I read, the more cut to the quick I am by what I imagine their pain to be. Maybe because my loss of Sarah is so fresh, I am touched by what Adam and Eve lost, and I grieve for them. My heart is also aware of what the whole of humankind lost when our ancestors were ripped apart from the joy which was God's only intention. My heart breaks again, and it breaks for all of us. It's all so sad.

Pushing past my sadness, which now is an increasingly difficult task to achieve; many other reflections come to mind. I remember all of the insecurities and fears that hovered around my preaching. I was terribly self-conscious. They say that public speaking is the greatest, the most common fear that most people carry. For many people, the fear of public speaking surpasses even death. I have been terrified by both and I think death still takes the cake, but even so, preaching remained a necessary evil which I was forced to endure.

I endured the preaching and the fears that it triggered by putting my best foot forward, but fear and embarrassment was never far from the surface. It was not that I couldn't have improved if I had just humbled myself a little bit and reached out for help. My pride wouldn't allow that.

I remember being invited to a group of local pastors who met together for the purpose of practicing sermon development and delivery, but I was not willing to admit to myself—let along anybody else—that my skill set might not have measured up to what was required of me. I ran away from most opportunities for improvement and, instead, became good at hiding. I could cover up my inadequacies, but I could not shake the fear that someday I would be exposed as a fraud. The fear of being exposed as a fraud was an anxiety that my experiences with Meg would only serve to deepen.

Plagued by these insecurities and others, I remember being really anxious to see Meg the next time we met. I think that I was afraid each time I saw her. This session would be no different than the others in that way.

I was always anxious to see Meg, but I was anxious around many people, so that was nothing new for me. What I was not accustomed to, was fishing for compliments. It was not my style to be so overtly emotionally desperate. I was surprised then, that while Meg was still in the process of sitting down, I blurted out, "So, did you like my sermon?" I had lost any semblance of cool. As I listen to the recording of this session, I can literally hear the figurative drool of desperation dribbling down my chin. Also, I still don't like the sound of my voice.

"Well", she said, "I thought that, if sermons had credits like they put on the end of movies, I should have at least been given co-writer, co-producer status". The twinkle of in her eyes seemed to suggest that she was kidding, but I was never really sure with her. She continued, "But actually, maybe because my fingerprints are all over what you said, I thought it was the best sermon that I'd ever heard. I'm sure you must hear that all the time though".

"Well yeah, I guess I do." I lied; I rarely got any of the credit that I craved for from my congregation, and I am especially suspicious of a compliment from Meg. I also was confused why she thought that she deserved credit for my sermon, where was that coming from?

Regardless, all that it took was a half-sincere, sarcastic throwaway line from Meg and my ego needs had been fed enough. With my pride's appetite temporarily abated, the hungry beast went back to its cage, but it was only a moment before it would come roaring back. In the meantime, I smiled with contentment and waited.

"Did you have another dream?" she asked. Now it was my turn to be coy. For the first time that day, I felt myself to be on somewhat equal footing with her. I saw the hunger in her eyes, not for me the man, but for the message I could give. It was the dreams which were the hook for Meg. An ego-less man would have been blessed by His gift of generosity given, but my pride felt the power rush of long delayed gratification. I wanted to be the focus of the genius, not the dreams. I waited until her eyes pleaded even more urgently for my words. In the absence of true confidence, emotional gamesmanship was required to cover my fears, so games were what I played.

"Why, did you get something out of the dream, something out of the sermon? Do you like the way I my voice sounds, did I have you on the edge of your seat?" My words had tipped the creepy meter in the wrong direction. If I didn't know any better, I would think that this is some kind of misguided, grossly ineffectual attempt to be charming.

I'm suddenly suspicious of my own emerging sliminess that seems to be bubbling to the surface too often. *What was happening to me? Who was I? I'm not the creepy guy, I'm not the guy with a wandering eye, and I'm not the one who wears his emotional neediness on his sleeves. I'm cool (kinda), I'm nice. Why had she gotten under my skin so quickly?*

She looked me square in the eye and said, "Yes, I got a lot out of your dreams and sermon. The way things work with me is that I swing to the light but darkness seems to pull me back after a while, and then I swing again. It's exhausting and I'm frustrated by it. The dream has so much beauty in it; it swung me in the direction of the light. I stayed there for a longer time than I'm used to.

"It's like the dream tipped the scales in the favor of the good in me, the way I want to be. The dream talks of unrealized potential and being awakened to something familiar and yet new. I like that. It resonates and gives me hope, hope which I am not accustomed to feeling. I know that this sounds presumptuous, but I think that when the woman was talking to you in the dream, I think she was actually talking to me as well."

What Meg said freaked me out more than a little, and that's saying a lot, because I was already on the cusp of freak-out — and being freaked out was not my typical stance in life. The unsettling thing was what she said about the dreams being for her as much as for me. This was actually a passing thought that had occurred to me earlier that morning, but I had dismissed it as being too strange. Heaven speaking to me was strange enough, but then to be spoken through... to some strange woman... was too much. I didn't want something so personal to me to be so closely linked to someone else. Meg being a direct part of my Heaven dreams would be too much sacredness shared, too much intimacy offered. I was walking on uneven ground, so I shut down and shadowed the beginnings of a thousand thoughts and feelings.

Sadly, part of my way of performing my duties as pastor involved the ability to put up a false front when needed. I had always told myself that I would summons up my false front only for the benefit of others. If I could alleviate the suffering of a parishioner by presenting more hope, more certainty, than perhaps the situation warranted, then so be it. This was one of the few times that I was aware of when I put on those "pastoral airs" not to attend to the fears of another, but to my own. So, I pulled back emotionally, I held my posture as one accustomed to be taken seriously. I used my "sermon voice" to convey the status that I didn't feel.

I saw myself as hiding behind my clerical robes even though as a non-denominational church pastor, I wouldn't be caught dead wearing a robe. Wrong vibe for me, too religious. Evangelicals are free from such elitism, and pretense. At least I had thought so; I was now discovering as pretense of a different order. As the lead pastor of a moderately successful Church, I was riding the heights of professional promise. Yet here was the truth that I couldn't avoid, I was beginning to see the depths of just how little substance I had to share. I had to fake it, I had to pretend that my spiritual acumen was at least at Meg's level.

A corner had been turned; I was no responding to Meg more than she was responding to me. She now held the power; she was now the lead partner in our little dance. But I kept my professional face on and forced my insecurities down, and it worked, in its own kind of way. I felt better, but Meg seemed to be adversely affected. I saw that as I puffed myself up with my supposed professional authority, that she deflated. It was like a game of emotional teeter-totter, as I pushed myself up, she went down. Fear and insecurity became the energies that we were passing like a hot potato back and forth.

She had a hard time sitting still; her eyes darted around, looking for a ledge to land on. Her normally cool demeanor had melted into a red hot mess. I felt guilty that my false-self had such a toxic effect on her, but not guilty enough to lower my shields.

It seemed weird to me that, during most of my time with Meg, I couldn't access the wisdom and the peace which the dreams had sent to me. Outside these sessions, the dreams impacted me; I could carry their spirit. With Meg, it was like we were in an alternate reality, where I had to thrash about without access to the eternal perspective that the dreams gave to me.

It was ironic that it seemed to be the messy chemistry between Meg and I that was the conduit, the trigger by which the dreams arrived, but apart from the times of actually telling her the dreams, I could not benefit from the beauty of the dreams when I was with her. Too often, alone with her, I was left to my own earthly devices.

I remained, for a brief time, calm and cool, measured and patient. I summoned up my best empathic fake face and inquired, "You seem to be a bit on edge. What's wrong?" She took a moment to acclimate to my voice and then once she found focus, we were off and running.

"I'm a book, just beginning and I hate it and love it," she said. "I feel pushed and pulled, punched, and pounded like someone is kneading me."

At first, I thought that she said "needing" me, like dependency. I was afraid that she could read my mind and could see just how much I wanted her approval, but thankfully I realized that what she was saying was the word "kneading," like the thing that a baker does to pizza dough. She is saying that she feels emotionally punched by this process, so I felt relieved that she is not clairvoyant. I was still on somewhat solid ground. I could also relate to, in my own way, the experience of being emotionally punched by this process.

I was just catching my breath, grateful for a landmine being dodged as Meg poured out the state of her life in graphic detail.

She showed her vulnerability, she told her story of loss. She told me the sad tale of how her mom left her and her dad when she was only seven. She never heard from her mom again, even when her beloved father died in a car crash when Meg was eleven. Suddenly orphaned, and not able to find any relatives able or willing to care for her, Meg was put into the foster care system, where she stayed until she ran away from her group home at age seventeen.

She recounted her ups and downs, her terror and her ecstasy. It all came out so raw, so full of scathing self-awareness and moral examination. She showed such spiritual awareness and insight. She had awareness that, despite all of my training and education, I couldn't touch. Spiritual directing, pastoral counseling... whatever you want to call it, it was not supposed to be a competition, but this one was, at least from my end. It was also a competition that I was losing.

I became humbled by her vulnerability. She had the gift of *real*. She also had a disarming style of describing trauma in a matter of fact kind of way. I was tempted to dismiss her emotionally capacity as one who is detached or aloof, but every time that I was confident in my amateur diagnosis, Meg would descriptively tell me of how these events impacted her very soul and I sat in awe. She shared herself with profound authenticity, self-awareness, and faith.

Instead of being inspired by her realness to dip my own toes into the pool of transparency and faith, all I could feel was envy. My brief moment of profound respect for her had morphed, or better said, disintegrated into idealization. I heard a voice in my heart whispering something about the valley of the shadow of death, but I couldn't focus. I was mesmerized by her edgy dance of dark and light. I wished that I had half of her depth and dimension. I wondered how it was that someone could be so emotionally aware at such a young age.

This time, Meg did read my mind, she stopped talking, glanced up with a hint of her own snarky smile and said, "Got to pay your dues if you want to sing the blues and you know it don't come easy." I was floored.

I had to pay my dues, I had to struggle and suffer the truth if I wanted to catch even a whiff of the realness which Meg owned. I couldn't bounce over or around the necessary steps. I had to begin with the painful awareness of the substance which I lacked and not hide behind the degrees displayed on my office walls. If I want to walk the King's highway of faith, I have to pay at the toll gate, and that payment would hurt.

In my state of envy of Meg, I continued to ascribe to her magical and mystical qualities. How did she know to quote Ringo Starr and the "You know it don't come easy" song to me? I had even once thought about doing a sermon on the life of the Apostle Paul using the "Got to pay your dues" lyric as the title. How did she know? She instinctively knew the incalculable distance between the thoughts which tickled the imagination of my brain and the immaturity of my soul. Off and on, she had the unnerving ability to look into my soul and diagnose my condition and then prescribe the treatment plan needed to treat this condition. No one else had ever done that to me, and I had never even considered any soul treatment necessary, but all kind of new possibilities were awakening.

The dreams, the window into Heaven seemed to bring the aura of the paranormal into all parts of my life. Maybe Meg was part of a divine plan to bring me transcendence. Or maybe not, maybe it was just an intuitive impulse on her part. Regardless, even now, I probably still romanticize and overstate her capacities.

I remember random thoughts ebbing and flowing in my brain. One second I dismiss Meg as wacko, the next I elevate her to savant. I didn't know what to think, I couldn't find any consistency or middle ground to the conflicting voices in my head. I was singing two songs at once and there was no harmony, no rhythm, and they are both off key.

What I do know is the voice of God, the voice of truth, and I know when His sweet voice is speaking in my ear. He spoke in heart whispers, soft, but of an undeniable quality... easy to discern. The voice that He spoke into my heart was saying, "You will receive much good from her, you will receive exactly what you need from her in due time." But, another voice in my head was translating my heart's message into something more like, "Meg is who you need in order to find your way in life, without her, you will stay forever stuck, frozen, and a nobody."

My guess now would be that the second voice was not the voice of God, but the voice of fear and pride. The second voice was a voice which was lacking in faith and void of discernment. Sadly, in the moment, I am more swayed by the voice of the desperate and dark than the voice of the Divine.

I was shocked and ashamed to feel as if I needed her. I knew that these dynamics were all wrong. It's not right for a pastor to have spiritual need of one whom he is called to shepherd. I remember thinking that I should stop meeting with her, it was not right. But I rationalized that she seemed to be benefitting from our time together. I shouldn't pull back from something just because it was hard. I thought that I just had to "man-up" and do my job.

I also rationalized that if I ever wanted to do my job well, I would need more edge to my personality. I saw that Meg had something about her which was real; a part of her was flavored by something other than vanilla. I saw myself as milquetoast in comparison. Nice and well-intended was the best of what I had to offer, and I was sickened by the thought of that. I told myself that my time with Meg would be a teaching experience, that I would grow emotionally by giving her spiritual direction, that I would be a better pastor, a better man, even a better husband by continuing to counsel her. But no matter how I couched my motivations with rationalization, I was drawn to her and I justified it, and I knew that it was wrong.

My thoughts were drifting to the dark edge of wrong. Every wrong has just the right amount of right. The right which Meg inspired was genuine self-examination. It was true, being with her had caused me to look at my life like I had never done before, and I wasn't impressed by what I saw. I had weighed myself in the balance and found myself wanting.

While these thoughts had some elements of humility, there were corresponding elements of risk. For example, I found that the less favorably I looked at myself, the more that I elevated her in my mind. I had a hard time sitting with the irrefutable evidence of my limitations; it was much more scintillating to put Meg on a pedestal. I much preferred to see her as exceptionally special rather than accept that in many ways, I was not.

The problem was that idealizing Meg was fraught with its own dangers. My curiosity about her, a mild infatuation with her, was beginning to wander into darker, seedy places, taking sips from the poisoned cup of obsession. I didn't even notice that I liked the taste.

As I look back now, I wonder if I ever really treated her as the real person that she was. Initially, I had dismissed her as weird, but now I idealized her as "The way, the truth, and the life." The truth is that neither my judgment of her nor my idealization of her did justice to who she actually was.

Regardless of the maze of convoluted thoughts, at the end of the day I still wanted to impress her. Looking to give her something of worth, I told her of the second dream which had come to me the night before. Maybe that wish to impress her was not a good motivation, but I always found solid ground when I leaned on my dreams. Without these dreams, I would have been utterly lost. They gave a structure to my life, a hope which served me so well in the midst of my emotional chaos and confusion. These dreams were interesting at a time when I felt that everything about me was bland. I felt that life had conspired against me to keep me relegated to the ranks of the terminally boring, but the dreams at least gave my life a little flavor.

So, I turned to the dreams, and again they came to my memory verbatim. I spoke them out directly, without explanation or commentary. This was the second dream, but it was really a continuation of the first. The two dreams blended seamlessly, and I was drawn into, once again, the mind, heart, and soul of a woman on a heavenly journey.

Even now, I am grateful now for the tape playing of the dreams; listening to myself tell the dream gives me the words which I had lost. Even though I had forgotten the words, I never totally lost the pictures, they imprinted on my soul. Too often I forgot to open this most precious of gifts, but somewhere inside, I knew that I could at any time close my eyes, open my heart and see places steeped fully in the Divine. The pictures were infused with healing. These are the words which I shared with Meg in an attempt to do justice to the places that I saw. This is the telling of the second dream.

CHAPTER FIVE

"*Off in the distance, a solitary church bell rang. The bell toned in unison with a rhythm in her soul. Sacred notes reverberated with life and love and she was incapable of resisting their healing energy, even if she wanted to. After a long time of being soulfully altered, she drew back from the purity of what was pulsating in her and around her. She loved it all; she was amazed and filled with joy, but ill-equipped to do anything other than just digest it. She doesn't feel rushed in any of this; she intuitively knew that this beauty wasn't going anywhere. This beauty stands unchangeable, uninterruptible, and forever. She was reminded again that she is home.*

She again looked across the valley where the effervescent stream ran, wild and free. Her eyes slowly took in the sights and then rose up to higher ground. There was a plateau of land across from her, flattening out after a steep rise of cliffs. The dream traveler saw an ancient monastery which she knew to be the source of the simple, sacred chiming. It was the chiming which was setting the course of rhythm within her.

The ringing of the bell continued to do its work. The bell's deep timbre stirred in her an awakening of her soul to song. She heard the song that this world sings, the song that the world sings to its Creator. The song of this world is a song of praise, adoration, and gratitude. It remains woven into the fabric of this place like the medieval scene was woven into the fabric of the tapestry.

If she had been capable previously of hearing a dozen notes of melody and harmonies in her prior existence, she could now discern an infinite number of notes with endless variation, but all of them, always singing the simple truth of God's beauty, capacity, greatness, and love.

Their song lifted her up in rapture; the melodies of worship were so sweet, so complex and nuanced, so simple and true. Praises lifted up to the Lord, and His pleasure answering back. All was song, all was ease, all was beauty. Countless voices, countless weavings of melodies and notes became one intoxicating song. She smiled with all of her being, she breathed from the top of her head to the bottom of her feet. Her body felt seamless, each part embracing other parts like best friends. She stood for an eternity, lost and found in the joy in and around her. She was ready to move, ready for adventure to come.

Her awareness eventually stirred again within her and she oriented herself back to the dwelling. She became aware of the presence of others there with her. She was slightly taken back to see three living lions standing before her. Each lion, in line, was more regal than the next. They had transformed from the living tapestry to real, breathing, majestic beings. They were strong, huge, and fierce. The woman could see the sheen of sweat on their backs, smelled the dry dust of the savannah on their skin. It was the perfume of the wild.

Every pore of the lions' beings poured out to her their sacred intention, their acceptance and respect, and their loyalty to her. They conveyed that they were content to stand with her forever, and that they were blessed to bless her and her journey. The saying that "the rich get richer" took on a fresh meaning to the dream traveler. She was truly rich, and getting indescribably richer.

Her mind could almost see parts of the journey ahead; she saw enough to know that there were others on this journey with her. There was a slight tingle of energy which vibrated like a hummingbird, just past her ear. There was something else alive in her room... invisible but present.

Ever so slowly, she was beginning to anticipate some of the rhythms of this new world. It wasn't shocking then when, like a perfectly orchestrated theatre production, an invisible curtain was drawn back and two angels stepped forward.

They, too, were now with her and, like the lions, they came from the tapestry, what I was coming to know as "her tapestry," a foundational piece of herself—come to life.

She now easily accepted the realness of this living tapestry. She easily accepted that something innate like tapestry could breathe and move, her mind was not shocked that beings could move in and out of its scenery. Things unimaginable in her prior existence became common place in her new life.

As breathtaking as the tapestry was, the angels were the beings which captured her full attention. The angels were exquisite. They appeared delicate, a thousand whispering leaves of gold, shimmering with devotion, purpose and power. She immediately loved them. She stared at them forever, and was unendingly moved by their beauty. She smiled because she couldn't get over their graceful different-ness. She noticed that they appeared to be walking, when they were actually flying, and when they appeared to be flying, they were actually walking. Her mind couldn't fully grasp what she saw, so she just smiled like an adolescent in love and accepted these new realities.

It only remains for the wise man of her tapestry to join this fellowship. The wise man was a great comfort to the dream traveler. The wise man was the first, seemingly, of her own kind that she had seen in this world. The man had sweet, smiling eyes and he personified in his face the dichotomy of the ancient youthfulness, a quality which was so present in this place. These qualities of forever wise, forever young were characteristics, especially clear to see, amongst those in her travelling party.

A LIFE in the DAY of HEAVEN

All in this world presented itself as simultaneously both old and new, and this too, has a soul-altering effect. She had first thought herself dead, now she thought of herself as born, and she couldn't decide whether she was old or young, so again, she just shrugged and smiled.

So, the six (three lions, two angels, and a wise man), who the woman now called her companions, stood before her, patient and relaxed. Their very posture spoke that they were there solely for her. In a world without threat, without conflict, without interruption of all things beautiful, they provided further shelter and covering to her. If possible, the woman relaxed even more, and the depth of her soul again opened up to receive the good all around her.

Stairs lead down, outside of her new home. She followed stone pavers laid out before her through terraces of beautiful gardens. Being outside was unsettling, so once again she was afraid to stop and look at the beauty, now close enough to be touched. The world has invited her to adventure, but she hesitated, and for a moment the woman searched for her familiar tapestry of color. Following a flitting moment of dismay, she remembered her companions. It was the lions who grounded her, who reassured her, who emboldened her to venture out.

Her companions were her tapestry, come to life, and what an arsenal they presented. Strength within her has been summoned by the lions so she moved forward, her eyes on the powerful haunches of the lead lion. Still, she felt afraid she would lose her nerve, so she rushed quickly through formal gardens of the house, barely registering the colorful nuisances of shadow and light, the amazing orchestras of scent. She wanted to get away from the gardens, they felt claustrophobic to her, and she wanted to get into the open space of natural air, and color and light.

It took her only a short time to acclimate. At first, she had a fear that perhaps there would not be enough air for her to breath outside of her new home, away from her tapestry. She found that she breathed easily, and that there was plenty of *space and air around her and in her. Everything, in fact, was easy, there was no strain. She slowed down and checked an internal antenna, an antenna that she had never consciously realized she carried with her. This antenna was not one of her new potentials which had been activated, but a carry-over from her previous world, and she was surprised that she had not seen it before. She was beginning to suspect that in the absence of any true security in the previous world, she had no ability to see all of the layers of fears and self-protection mechanisms that she had created and maintained.*

Regardless of what once was, her antenna now could find absolutely no threat of any kind. It searched, but found no threat here. In fact, what the antenna did find was not just the absence of anything fearful, but the strong presence of utter safety and security. Not just an absence of shadow, but the presence of non-ending light. Not having any purpose in this place, the antenna shriveled up like a balloon whose air is suddenly released and the antenna squirted off into the abyss.

The woman fully exhaled and it was as though all of her fears blew out of her. As she walked, she found that she was rapidly losing her ability to fear. She began to wonder, like an elderly person trying to remember whether they had already taken their pills at night, she began to wonder whether she had ever had any fears at all.

Now completely relaxed, the woman stopped to take inventory of what she had rushed by. She was amazed by the color of the terraced gardens she has walked through. Their colors are rich, vibrant, and alive. She surveyed what she did not see from her hillside home, but was now in her line of sight.

She saw that the river ran close to, but did not connect with, a small lake just to the right of its path as it flowed to the sea. The lake, or large pond, looks dark, deep, and clear. She noticed a half-moon spread of sand lined the portion of the lake directly below her. Pine trees surrounded the lake, dark green and full along the shore, becoming scrubbier as the trees thinned out towards the sandy beach of the ocean beyond. She stopped to soak in the beauty.

The sun warmed her, strong and soft, devoid of anything harsh or toxic. All was alive, all was perfect around her. Angels soared above her, golden auras of light. Their songs cascaded through her, infusing her with capacity for gratitude and praise. She delighted in God, delighted in His creation, and found herself wondering at the countless other worlds of creation of which He presided. How many other places and spaces might be as perfectly aligned with beauty as this? She felt God's delight with her, rebounding back, which gave her unspeakable satisfaction and wonder.

The Presence of God's heart provided too many attack points of beauty for her to resist and she drifted into a reverie of ecstasy. She would not tone down her joy, she would not meter out her pleasure like a miser, handing out pennies to the poor. No, and she rode her joy with fierce abandon. It was a long, life-embracing ride.

When she slowly brought herself back to her environment, she found her companions continuing to stand patiently at the ready. They took what the woman will come to describe as "journey formation." The largest lion took the front and the remaining two lions stood on each side of the heaven traveler. The angels hovered above and the wise man followed from behind. They were off again.

The path moved to the right of her house, and the lake below quickly moved out of her immediate sight. They walked through orchards of fruit trees, fragrant with ripe fruit. She paused, hesitated, and then took a bite of an apple from a beautiful tree. Suffice it to say that the taste was so much better than anything she had ever known. She simply accepted this blessing with what was becoming her ever-present gratitude.

She gave simple thanks, partially because gratitude now flowed from her like an exhaled breath, and partially because she knew no other meaningful response to beauty. Her old world was no longer her point of reference, and she was content to forget and let this new world elevate her.

The ground beneath the traveler's feet was soft but firm, a bit spongy and completely comfortable. The ground also felt alive as all things did in this world. The ground breathed and moved in rhythm with her. She found that the ground has a language as well and spoke to her up through the soles of her feet. The ground spoke to her the path she would take. She felt like the Australian Aborigines must have felt in her old world, following songlines in the ground, linking points both of destination and destiny.

She walked in perfect balance, not only in balance within herself, but in balance with everything around her. Every part of her was whole, no competition or conflict. She felt the same seamless connection with everything else alive around her. She was solid, grounded, yet light.

She moved up and down hillsides of flowing grasslands and majestic oak trees. She could see forever...rows of grapevines, growing in symmetrical order up and down hills and valleys. The vineyards were in perfect harmony with the contour of the hills. They blended perfectly with the natural order of things.

The harmonious blending of beauty brought back to her mind the joy of the song ever-present around her. She tuned into the songs of God-worship and joined in with the singing. Always song, always singing, all things, all beasts, all trees, all men and woman, all angels and planets. She became more nurtured each time her feet touched the earth, enhanced by each beam of sunlight and uplifted by each breath of wind.

There was a turn of the path down towards a valley of green. The woman moved with grace and elegance, effortlessly. She stopped to look, to see, to breathe. The sun warmed her skin, always soft like the sweetest of mornings. Freshness enveloped her, and the continual tingling sensations of air, scents, and flavors played with her on the breeze. She had walked forever, without fatigue, fast enough to enjoy all things new with wondrous vigor, slow enough to savor.

A LIFE *in the* DAY *of* HEAVEN

She wondered about many things. Mindful of her prior place of living, she remembered people and events, but the memories were all seasoned with freshness and healing. Her mind and soul and eyes always smiled. Her face might not have shown it, but everything in her and about her was a smile. She felt completely content. She did not suffer, there was no burden, but she did wonder about things, about people she remembered as she walked, as she smiled.

The path turned steeper as it wound down towards the valley floor. She had no doubt that she was on the right path, walking in the right way, prescribed for her at precisely the right time, in precisely the right way. She was curious as the path converged into just a narrow opening and ended at the base of a doorway.

The round door now directly in front of her was about her own height and was very thick and solid. It looked like what you might think of as an entrance to a hobbit house. Like all things in this world, the door showed itself to be sturdy and safe; it spoke to her, not as a barrier, but a point of demarcation. She sensed that the door spoke a truth that whatever was behind it was good and beautiful, and would be of a different quality than the place where she now stood.

She sensed that whatever was on the other side held a gift for her. All things that she had seen and felt and heard were things that she had received as gifts, but whatever was behind the door would be intensely personal. The thought emerged that she was free to open the door whenever she wanted, and that the opening of the door would be like the opening of her heart. Opening the door would come from the power of her own volition, an act of will, birthed in beauty, nurtured in security, lifted in laughter.

This heavenly traveler saw that the door was hers to open, like seeing a Christmas present under the tree, with her name written on it. But like a Christmas present which she knew was hers, she still must open it at the right time, and in the right way. She was not to open this gift alone. She must open it in the presence of the Giver, the opening must be shared.

She paused to hear the birds sing.

The birds sat on branches of tall trees that she could see as growing from the other side of the door. It occurred to her that the singing of the birds was the one thing in this new divine place which was exactly the same as the world from when she came. All of the other colors, sounds, and sights were exalted versions of what she knew in her old life. The bird songs sounded exactly the same, and she wondered why she did not recognize their beauty before.

She took her time; it truly was her time to take. Things moved at a leisurely pace in her and around her. There was no rush. She could walk away from the door if she was not ready. She could go back on the path that she was on, and that would be okay. She stood, a little uncertain as to what she wanted to do. She had been more passive up to this point, taking the direction of her companions, and moving in pace with the vibrations of the songlines from the ground, but now she felt that she was being invited to actively partner with this world.

This world is her friend, God is King, and yet to move open this door required an exercise of her will. The message came to her again, almost audibly this time, and it said, "The opening of this door is like the opening of your heart, the choice is yours."

Never having had the pleasure of a truly open heart as a basis of comparison, she realized that it never occurred to her to consider her heart as being so closed off. The barriers that guarded her are just coming evident to her. Just as a fish takes wetness for granted, so had she had assumed that the closed condition of her heart was the only condition available to her, the only condition that she would ever know.

Her heart has responded to all of the treatments which this new world provided. Her heart has been steadily bathed in safety, thrilled by wonder, cleansed by waters, made soft by beauty, and now it yearned for more room to breathe. Once again, she considered the door. The door was beautiful in its own right, but she could now see that it could, in fact, act as a barrier if she allowed it to. It was a barrier, but it was a barrier easily opened, all it took was just a subtle shift, a willingness to trust.

The world held its breath, not for fear, but for buildup of anticipation over the corner about to be turned. A power was about to be released. The woman waited. She has become wise enough not to force her own will apart from the all-pervasive power which she can feel here. She wanted to act, but yet she knew to wait. She would not impulsively tear the wrappings off the gift.

She was humbled to know that the wonder and power around her was responsive to her process, intune to her level of readiness. The new world and its blessings were something which she was to simply receive with patience and reverence. She stayed on full alert, ready for a breakthrough, and also aware that the power to move the door open, has not yet been given to her.

She began to learn life's true power here; she felt its intoxicating effect. From this knowledge, the woman chose to see this world for what it was. It was a vehicle of transformation, like all of life is. It is an instrument of beauty, a cup to be drunk from. It is a canvas for God to paint. The world is something from which she can and does harvest the sacred fruit of her own personal redemption, renewal, and re-birth, but a gentle suspicion was arising in her. The suspicion was that everything here was truly His story, for His glory. She knew that no matter how high beauty had elevated her, it was He who was most high and lifted up, and that this was precisely as it should be.

She continued to stand before this door of choice. The task for the dream traveler was no longer about forcing the door open; the choice was more about intentionally aligning with the world in just the right way to be partnering with its power. The choice was neither to observe the new world, nor to take dominion over it, but to merge with this world, and the Creator who created it. God, Beauty, His will, her freedom to choose, *all were to move together in an ancient dance of liberation and transformation.*

She drank in the world around her, not just for pleasure, but for power. Not her power, but its power... His power. The power was not loud and heavy, but soft, sweet, and soothing. It had been there all the time; she just couldn't see it. She had always thought that power would be more like an explosion than a whisper, something to tackle and tame, like a wild horse, rather than the soothing, comforting voice of an old friend.

She wondered again at how much she had missed about life's truths. How strong could soft and kind and gentle be? Soothing thoughts, sights, sounds and people had their place in her former life, and although they might be nice for a while to look at and to listen to, at some point one has to move on to tough, and angry, competitive and direct to get things done. Right?

She had known all along that the soothing that this world gave to her was there for her to feel better, but what she hadn't seen before was that the soothing power also existed for her to be better, to be powerful in her own right, to be healed, to become whole, and to rise up to her God-given stature.

She tuned down her past perceptions. She dialed into the softness of the breeze, the quiet of this place, the seemingly smallness of her breath. She turned her attention to the door and was quiet. Curious about what was on the other side... she wanted to know, but she was content to wait.

For the third time, the truth came in a whisper that the closed door was her closed heart, her heart closed to God. She knew that all that would be available to her beyond the door would be good, and true, and right. She also knew that by opening her heart, she would be losing a lot. She would lose her right to see herself as being center stage. The woman knew that what lay behind her closed heart would be wildly successful, but she also knew that this, in some tangible way, will not be fully her story, at least not as the person that she had known herself to be.

A LIFE in the DAY of HEAVEN

Much like the simple way that she'd slipped from her old world to this new world, the transformation happened without fanfare, drumroll, or drama. She looked at the door and saw it now, not as solid, but more like the reflection of water on an utterly still lake. She saw a cloudy image of a woman who she believed to be a representation of her own good self, just further along in the journey. She smiled at a sweet joke that only she can see and hear, she lowered her heart shields and stepped beyond.

Stepping through the door, she entered into a new place, a new space. The energy here had a different quality, quieter and gentler than where she had just been. Everything was a bit muted and diffused. It lacked the heart-racing "pop" of color, sight, and sound of the space on the other side of this door. The light filtered down, seasoned with soft, pale colors. The word "timeless" came to mind.

The woman understood that this was an important place for her. It was a place which contained connections that lay at the foundation of her relationship with, and to, life. The thought of connections made her think of the tapestry, hanging at the place she now considered as being her home. She thought that this new space that she'd entered into was like the reverse side of the tapestry. Her thoughts confirmed themselves as she journeyed here.

This place would contain insights into all of the weavings which had stayed invisible to her, up until this point. The relationships, the interconnections of seemingly random lessons and attitudes were front and center here. The color of events and circumstances were on the flip side of her attention, and she retained her connection with her life as she understood it to be, but the threads and fabric were beginning to reveal patterns, patterns which fascinated her. She wondered if her entire life had been a purposeful artistic expression, and not the random, mundane, misuse of energy she had always assumed it to be.

Like anyone viewing the reverse side of a tapestry, she saw that it was not possible to clearly discern the picture on the other side. The threads of attitude, of character, presented a colorless, blurred picture. She knew that without the connections tied together on the back, without the bond of truth and life experience, without the character of her being, none of the beauty on the front would hold together.

Nevertheless, she missed the colors of the art that could be enjoyed on the front. She missed the drama and emotional impact of seeing the picture. She couldn't help but be impressed by the intricacies of the design; the attention to detail, the complexity of connections made that only can be seen looking at the tapestry's reverse side... but she was ready to move on.

She might not have been able to piece together all of the parts, but each piece was profoundly meaningful to her and she understood the events of her life in that highly personal way that only she could know. The underside, which she was seeing then, convinced her that the pieces all fit together, and have been woven together in a thoughtful and creative way. She wanted to feel pride in this—but she, again, knew the truth that she was not the artist, and that her dignity was founded on the truth that she, herself, was a work of art uniquely and wonderfully made.

In this place of diffused light and muted colors, she was drawn to the sparkle of light and color on the horizon. She thought of a song once enjoyed, "I looked at life from both sides now, win and lose and still somehow, it's life's illusion I recall, I really don't know life at all." She smiled because, although the reverse side, the unseen side of weavings, threads and fabrics, has moved her greatly, she was still drawn to color. She could appreciate that the unseen was where the actual work was done, the unseen was where the connections were made and maintained; it's the unseen that made the beauty possible. Although she knew that it was the hidden that allowed the vibrant pictures to exist, she can't resist the visible, the allure of color.

As these thoughts moved through her mind, colors began to spread out before her, and she felt herself crossing another threshold. She stepped into a picture from her past. She was in a park, a place where she went to play as a young girl. The park was sweet and kind, and easy on her soul. She remembered a caretaker's house, where she would spend time with a grandfatherly type man who was her friend, an elderly man who tended to the maintenance and beautification of the park.

The caretaker's house was still there, a simple home, but one of dignity, form and function. Stepping into this home flooded her with memories and she realized that this place represented the best that her time on earth had given her. She lingered in the house, watched the light beam stream in through the windows and the open door.

Prior to this flood of memory, the woman thought that beauty, real beauty had not been available to her prior to her passing. She realized now that that assumption was not true. This place, her park, was from the broken world. Her connection with the sweet gardener/caretaker was from the broken world, and that connection, still, was also good. Though when she was a little girl she lacked the words, she had been moved by the simplicity of an elegant man whose whole purpose seemed to be the betterment of life around him.

It was a simple beauty that she had forgotten. The park was a humble place that she, and many others, had quickly learned to rush by. She had never even let the old caretaker know what he meant to her. How could she, as a child, realize that whatever else she ran off after in her earth-life, nothing would ever replicate, quite live up to the simple beauty of this place and time? The beauty of this new world, this heaven spreading out before her was unmistakable, but it was not the first place in her existence where she'd known beauty.

She felt like she was sensing both sides of the tapestry simultaneously, she was seeing an invisible connection between two worlds. She suspected that there was much to learn here at this place. She wondered about what she would see next. She looked out the backdoor of the caretaker's house and saw the garden that she assumed was the one that her old friend once tended.

She walked out the backdoor, turned towards the house and bowed deeply as a sign of respect and gratitude towards the memory of the old man. The old man, who had been so patient with her, the old man who never made a big deal out of anything, the old man who simply and sweetly had just been there, the old man who first taught her to know goodness in life, and how to effortlessly receive it. Knowing the good in life was birthed by his quiet dignity.

The woman smiled at the thought that, even though she had been singing songs of love and praise towards the Creator, this was the time that she had first shown true reverence towards a person or a place. She simply noticed the thought, considered it to be ironic, and moved on.

The garden, she could now clearly see, was in a state of disrepair. She wondered how long since the old man had cared for it, but even as she considered this, she also realized that nothing in this new world moved with the rhythm or reason of her earth-life. The disrepair of the garden had a purpose beyond her common understanding. The woman was coming to see that everything in Heaven was designed to speak of God's loving and healing heart specifically expressed to her. Taking comfort in these insights, the woman rests and takes in the special feel which the garden offered her.

She thought back over the last part of her journey. She had moved out from the other side of the tapestry, but the muted, hushed quality of quiet remained. The other side of the tapestry was different; there was a different type of perfection, of meaning there. She had seen the undeniable evidence of a supernatural Hand which had spun together the complexities of how her life. The genius of how all things had been woven together were almost too much for her to digest.

The woman was more comfortable in the garden. It was not sharp and precise and detailed like the connections seen on the other side of the tapestry, but it was warm and real, like an old friend. Even though the garden is in a state of begin neglect, there was still a strong quality of beauty there, a beauty not yet fully realized. The quiet of permanence she spoke to her, the physical force of stillness came over her and the garden gently sings songs of eternity into her heart. All is well with her soul. She smiled and continued her rest.

As she drifted off in some kind of trance/sleep, I woke up."

I had relived my personal journey in the retelling of this, the second dream. It was no small feat to even recognize where I was now back in space and time.

CHAPTER SIX

I sat in the silence, aglow in peace. For no reason that I can consciously connect with, I find myself saying out loud, "I have no more of the dream to tell, no more words to say. I woke up in rest. It was with the whisperings of eternity in my ear that my dream, for that night, had stopped."

It took me several minutes to get my bearings of where I was and what I was doing. I had become lost in the reliving of the eternal. At first I didn't realize where I was, I couldn't quite get my mind around that I was still in my office.

Having been so immersed in my experience of Heaven left me devoid of fear and pretense, it was hard to return to a world where my pride and envy was only a mistimed word or thought away. Even so, I shook my head hard to bring myself back to my Church office, back to my session with Meg.

Seeing Meg, realizing that I was so emotionally laid out before her, was a shock to my system. I had, through the telling of the dream, lowered my defenses in her presence. I never completely lost the conscious fact that she was the audience as I shared my dream—I needed to give Meg the benefit of this miracle, but I just wasn't ready for the intimacy of it all.

It certainly wasn't my intention, but due to the pure spiritual nature of mutually opening our hearts to Heaven, our souls were bonded in ways that I was not prepared for.

But even in that altered state of consciousness, I would be remiss to imply that Meg's impact on me, this brush with intimacy, was purely a function of sharing the dreams. She triggered me at a variety of levels. Her fearless directness scared me, her sarcasm delighted me, and her vulnerability impressed me. I was fascinated by her. She was madness, mirth, and muse, and I wanted a full measure of all. Even more disturbingly, I felt that I needed all of what she was able to give. I should have been content to bask in the delight of the divine of the dreams, but the wish of what I could have with a woman like Meg was suddenly taking precedent over what I my conscience and circumstances would dictate.

Looking at Meg, I continued to realize that we had been lost in our thoughts, in each other's presence, for a longer time than is socially appropriate, and a part of me enjoyed it. It remained a challenge to pull ourselves out of the beauty of timelessness, and the sweet connection between us. I battled within myself to pull myself out of this altered state of consciousness, but there seemed to be no way that I could snap out of my state and function in a conventional way.

I wasn't helped by the thought that I was, perhaps, falling in love with two women, neither of whom were my wife who I also loved. To further complicate things, one of these "not my wife" women was dead, but even that fact was murky, not exactly clear. Given what I was coming to know about Heaven and about my woman friend in Heaven, I wasn't even sure if I could carry on with my old understandings of what constitutes dead or alive. Was the woman in the Heaven dream dead? Not by any definition of dead that I could conjure up.

So, the lines of life and death were blurred. I guess that's a consequence of hanging out at the crossroad of Heaven and earth. But apart from that, all I knew was that both my spirit and my flesh were simultaneously fired up in ways that they had never been before. I was in love with the woman of Heaven, I knew her, and she knew me. Truth be told, I felt that I was her, and she was me. I had no defense, it was borderline unfair. Heaven had played matchmaker with my heart and I had no choice but to love her. The thing was that I my love for the woman of Heaven was pure and holy and there was no guilt in any of it, in light of everything else, I took comfort in that.

However unsettling it was to think that I could be falling in love with a dead woman, that was child's play compared to even the possibility that I could have seeds of such feelings for someone like Meg. On how many levels is this disgusting and wrong? Let me count the ways.

Blurred lines were becoming the dominant theme in my life and I wasn't happy about it. I ping ponged back and forth between my fascinations with Meg, which were tainted by foolishness, and the pure awe I felt towards the workings of God's holy hands. Not many, to my knowledge, had been privy to the presence of the miraculous of this type. These visits to Heaven were a gift, and I was determined to not look a gift horse in the mouth.

Pondering this mixture of profound and profane began to have a sobering effect on me as I sat across from Meg that day. My brain was clearing just enough to attempt to sort out what was going on. Where was I? Who was I? And just exactly who is this woman sitting across from me? Oh ya, it's Meg, she spells trouble for me, I should stay away.

These were clouded; half thoughts of an altered consciousness, but that didn't make them wrong. I wondered what she thought, what was going on in her head, but her thoughts were hidden to me; I could only hope that my thoughts were just as disguised to her.

I wondered if Meg had any idea of my thoughts and feelings. I wasn't a fan of this mind-reading capacity that she sometimes seemed to dabble in. I also prayed that her thoughts were of a higher caliber than mine. My spiritual mandate was to be the champion of safe and good, but I was slipping into the shadows of fear, pride, and want and I could only hope that I wasn't going to spoil a good gift given.

She suddenly focused and blurted out, "When I was a young girl, my father would take me fishing for trout in the Sierra Mountains. The trout we caught, we had to eat, nothing to waste. My Dad was skilled with knives and he could gut a fish, pull out all the bones, and have it ready to fry in a blink of an eye. That's what your dreams do to me. They gut me and fillet me with a flick of the wrist, the turn of a phrase. They open me up as sliced by the sharpest of knives."

"I'm sorry," I said. And I meant it. I was feeling generally guilty over everything, but especially the pastor in me felt guilty that the story that I gave to Meg to bless her was actually causing such slashing pain. I am to shepherd the sheep, not lead them to slaughter and butcher them with my words.

Not for the first time, she started a sentence with, "No, you don't understand." And then she clarified, "No cut has ever been so deep, so good, and so clean that it touches the wound. I need it to hurt. I just need it to continue to hurt good, and not hurt bad." I felt insecure whenever she accused me of not understanding her. She seemed to see me so clearly and it felt like we were playing a serious game and the cards were stacked in her favor.

I was confused, and when confused I should have just stayed quiet, but I was conflicted... out of sorts. I was realizing what a sheltered life I'd lived. I had never before felt even remotely dissatisfied about the privilege of security which life had afforded me. I had known the advantage in the certainty of predictability, but I was starting to feel ambivalent about the very advantages which I had drawn comfort from. Recently, my safe life felt more like a strait jacket than a security blanket.

Meg's life had been anything but sheltered, and I would never trade her life for mine, but her suffering and grittiness gave dimensions of life that I could not touch. I was afraid that my naiveté would look infantile in her eyes. I wanted to give her strength and depth, but I felt like a child afraid, a child afraid that he was not prepared for the task at hand.

"You're right, I don't understand." I tried to make that statement more of implication of her craziness, I wanted to put her in her place, but I only sounded like a childish whine, a voice too high-pitched, too shrill to make my selfish point with any gusto. I think my childish voice came out from a gnawing sense that Meg had been right all along, that she was right to speak of what was lacking in me.

True to what was truly good in her, she ignored my pettiness. Instead she did what she was best at; she used the openness birthed from the hearing of the dream to press further into her vulnerability. She told me more of her pain, she told of the dreadful horrors of her life. She also told the awful truth of how sweet her life sometimes was. Grace often sideswiped her just at the time when she traveled the intersection of broken—headed for destruction. He, God, always intervened and pointed her in the direction of redemption.

She told me of her salvation from God, His beauty interspersed with betrayals and dramas and traumas of life, some of which were created from the depths of her own foolishness. All of this, and more, had her constantly knocking at the door of God's purity and kindness. She would draw near to Him, ringing the doorbell of Heaven, only to dash away like a teenager pulling a childish prank.

She told me of how she would look back over her shoulder as He chased her. She could see His Light on the other side, but then the scene would shift and she slammed the door on her emotional hunger for Him. Because of the intensity of her need for Him, the stakes were too high, the risks were too great.

"It's the purity in Him crying out to the purity in me that I can't get traction with. He's there, I respond—but I stop myself, I'm afraid and... I don't know why. The shrinks that I see, say that it's my past, my abuses that have kept me from trust, and I'm sure that what they say has truth, but I think there's more to it. There is an inner blocking that I run up against.

The roadblock feels disproportionate to what I have suffered in childhood. This all feels, I guess, spiritual, some kind of suppression.

"There's a spiritual place that I just can't seem to get to. That's why I came to you, a pastor. You appreciate the spirit, the unseen world. You also are, well, noticeably impure, and I need that impurity too."

Meg was talking honestly about things I should have been an expert at, but my pride had been bruised with her "impure" remark. I was so easily offended. "Noticeably impure?" was all I could muster to say.

Meg seemed weary of all the ways that my ego could be so easily battered about. She sighed, "Yes, you lack purity, but that works for me. I've been around other Christians who have a purity that makes me clam up." "Oh," I countered, "you mean that they are too self-righteous for their own good, they're not real."

"No." Her words were weighted down by weariness as if she was the one doing all of the heavy lifting. "No, they are enlightened ones, people of faith and power, people who led me to salvation, but who don't mix well with my story. They are of the Spirit, they are expert, they are sky and I am ground. You have been touched by the Spirit, like I have, but you still have much rock, and sod, and clay in you. You are safe because you don't have a lot to offer, and because of that, you don't threaten me. I'm hoping that you have enough to offer to get me to another level, but I know you don't have too much to scare me off. There is comfort for me in that"

She was saying that my weakness made her feel safe. I was not a real man, a man whose strength might threaten her. How much more could my pride endure before fighting back? I was proud of myself that I hadn't lashed out at her before this point. I tried to tell myself that the truth was that I was so secure that I didn't need to defend myself. But that was baloney. I could feel my anger building up, like flood waters pressing on a dam, already spilling. Meg could see the blood rise in my face. She sighed deeply.

"I am healing, I can feel it," she said. "I am sorry. I am sorry that I don't have the energy to keep my darkness away, explain my story, accept my healing, and keep your ego fed all at the same time. You are helping me, let me help you. I will not play your drama game. I will not play the 'who is right, who is wrong, who is pure, who is not' game. I don't have the energy for it.

"You've been given a great gift, given these dreams. You did not create them, so just enjoy them. Don't let your ego make this about itself, and don't make this all about me, either. You are so possessive; you want to possess wisdom, just like you want to possess me. Wisdom is not for sale any more than I am. Please just enjoy it all. You fight for this right to be right—to be more right than me, but you can't win.

"If I lose then I die, if you lose you just lose a piece of your pride, something which would actually benefit you. You just go back to your wife and kids and career none the worse for the wear. So, here is your choice in our relationship, you can fight, you can try to be right, but you will lose. Your other option, the more desirable one, is to not fight me; don't make everything a power struggle. You decide, your ego or your satisfaction, because you can't have it both ways. You can't be both right and also on the right path with me"

Then she left. A second later, she knocked on the door. I expected an apology. Instead I get, "You know what would really help me?" she asked. "Can I get a copy of the part of our sessions when you tell the dreams?"

I saw no reason not to, so I called the church IT guy and I put him on it.

The sermon I spoke on Sunday poured out of the passion of spirit in me, inspired by Meg, inspired by the dreams of Heaven.

I saw my wife Sarah being especially fidgety that Sunday morning. She kept looking over her shoulder in Meg's direction, trying to get a read on who she was. I imagine that she was on the defensive, being protective. Given Sarah's trust and good nature, she probably saw Meg, whoever she was, as being more of a threat to me than any threat to herself. If protecting me from risk that was foremost in her heart, if Sarah saw me as more vulnerable than she was, then she was right.

Regardless of why Sarah was hyper-aware of Meg, the fact that she had Meg in her headlights disturbed me to no end. I didn't want Sarah to be bothered, I didn't want there to any type of tremor in the bond between us. I also didn't want Meg to be right that my supposed impurity could cause a betrayal of any kind, real or imagined. I wanted to protect my wife Sarah, but I also wanted to protect myself.

I remember a time when I was a kid; my mother went out to buy groceries. My brother and I were at home, doing what we mainly did in those days... fighting. One of us got thrown against an expensive lamp that my mom had just bought. The lamp shattered in pieces. My brother, being more intrinsically practical than I, ran upstairs to hide. Being the older one, I chose what I assumed to be the more elegant solution. I would head right into the eye of the storm. I would sit on the couch next to the lamp, reading my homework assignment from school. When my mom came back, I would pretend that I didn't notice the broken lamp and, when asked, I would offer the most plausible explanation that I could imagine, the dog did it.

I was holding my breath in the suspense of unleashing my flawless plan. My mom finally got home, and walked into the living room. She immediately suspected something amiss by the simple observation that I was doing my homework on a sunny afternoon. But in my mind I was home free; I casually looked in her direction, and ignored an impulse to look at the evidence of violent destruction. But instead of the air of benign indifference that I was going for, I strained to not look in the direction of the lamp.

Because of the physical and moral strain, I was holding my head stiffly as if my neck was in a brace locked in the chains of forced constraint. The smell of a rat filled my mother's maternal instinct empowered nostrils. Now on full alert, she looked in the direction of the broken lamp.

Without taking my eyes off of her I said, "It must have been the dog."

She said, "The dog was with me."

I said, "Maybe the dog (its name escapes me) did it before I got home."

"No," she said. "The only worse liar in this house than you is the dog, I would have known right away." Things spiraled downhill from there.

Anyway, that was the memory which my behavior triggered. I was trying to be cool, not a good look for me. My guilt would not allow my head to not turn anywhere near the direction of Meg. I hoped that Sarah did not possess the liar-alert gene that my mother had. I lied to my mother many times. Sarah's liar-detection gene muscle had rarely, if ever, been triggered by me; I prayed that it wouldn't be tested today.

The reality was that I had not done anything wrong. Except, except… and these are big exceptions, I had recently begun to think that there could be important life experiences that would only be available to me through a certain kind of connection with another woman. I was ashamed of those thoughts then, and, if anything, more ashamed now. I hungered for something deep, something to wake me out of my emotional and spiritual slumber. I wanted to be real good at what I did, and I justified any real or imagined intrigue with Meg as being a necessary first step in the process.

Even though Sarah had been a model pastor's wife, she did not push me, she did not pull in the direction of the raw and passionate faith that I was beginning to crave. It was a shock that I thought that Meg had gifts that my beloved Sarah could not give me. I remained deluded in thinking that to become the pastor I knew that Sarah wanted me to be, I needed what my time with Meg gave me. I continued to think that to reach my potential, I needed a weird mix of angel and demon that was Meg in my life. In hindsight, I deceived myself.

I was greatly relieved when, finally, it was time to step to the pulpit. It gave me the excuse of stepping out of the cauldron of drama that I was stirring in myself.

These were the sermon notes that I preached from, again arranged in a rough, informal order.

#1 THE TOXICITY OF PRIDE

Once softened, sweetened, and enhanced by the immensity of God's wisdom and beauty, there was no diluting that shot of personal pride that Adam and Eve coveted as the solution to their woes. They drank it straight up, no chaser. What choice did they have? Not much, by their accounting. They needed the thunderous roar of the ocean of God's might and love, but instead, they had an echo of former glory now corrupted and diminished.

Left to stand separate from the buffeting and temperance of God's Presence and blessing, Adam and Eve's pride was not the tonic they wished for, but rather a deadly toxicity which crippled the purpose for which they were created. This was not the satisfying flavoring that God-given personal self-worth was created for, but rather the trust put in pride had the beginnings of an intoxicating, impairing, life robbing addiction. Pride became a primary driving force in human life, something that our human species was not prepared to navigate. Pride and fear would deeply impair Adam and Eve's ability to accomplish their most fundamental need, the need to love God with their whole heart, mind and strength.

Pride's new role was to elevate its own importance, to create a continuing loop of narrative, justifying its own reason for existence. Pride's voice screamed power, but its fragility was revealed, its fake strength unveiled through pride's petulant entitlement, demanding retribution for the slightest of injury or threat.

Pride became equated with power for Adam and Eve; power was felt to be essential for their survival. God was equated, at some basic level, with abandonment and trauma. Adam and Eve still carried, and still passed down to their descendants, the potential for God's power within them to flame up from the embers of what once was, but compared to the roaring blaze of what was their connection with God in the garden, the embers felt too cold, too distant, so they were not stoked. What felt more immediate, what felt more reliable, was their own personal pride and their perceived capacity to create a rich live for themselves, rather than depend on God to give life to them.

There was much at risk here. Pride's existence was at risk as well. There was always the reality that if the host perished, then pride went with them. Pride was intimately invested in Adam and Eve's protection. The fate of Adam and Eve became intertwined with pride until it was hard to imagine their life without the promises pride made and the corresponding fear and guilt that pride was never able to distance itself from. As an act of survival, pride offered itself up as caretaker.

Pride seemed like it was all that was left of past power, past glory, past dignity. Pride was not like the serpent—its intention was not to destroy and deceive. It was empowered to be a protector, it was a survival partner, but it was in way over its head. It was a shadow promise, not capable, apart from God, of creating, sustaining, and expanding anything remotely resembling true life. It lived in the realm of wishes, nostalgic whispers, and empty promises. But it was there, it was something, it was present, and in the imagery of Tolkien's Lord of the Rings, it became "precious" to Adam and Eve.

Pride and Adam and Eve made a pact. In exchange for allowing space for pride to exist, Adam and Eve empowered pride to act on their behalf. The standards of pride, the power of pride, the expectations of pride, and the drama of pride must be a primary life force that Adam and Eve draw from. They must protect pride, pay attention to pride, draw it close, soothe it, draw comfort and familiarity from it as the special friend it was believed to be. Adam and Eve became as fiercely protective of pride as pride became of them. They promised to never leave or forsake one another, never to leave each other as they felt God had left them.

A LIFE *in the* DAY *of* HEAVEN

#2 ADAM AND EVE IN US

So where does that leave things now for us as the descendants of Adam and Eve? Christian theology has taught us that the stain of Adam and Eve's sin has been passed down from generation to generation, that their sin has become our sin. Their life experience, as the original human beings, has been passed down, copied if you will, into the emotional, physical, spiritual fiber of who we all are. A thought to consider, if remnants of Adam and Eve's DNA still pulsate in our own veins, could more of who Adam and Eve were be handed down to us as well. If we carry the disease that they activated, what else of their life experience also is transmuted over time and space?

Could it be, at least partially, that their God-given beauty is still active in our life experience today? Why not? Why would it be that only the sin was passed down from Adam and Eve's life experience? Why wouldn't the dignity, the wisdom, the fullness of faith expressive of God's original intent for us also remain? Why wouldn't the seeds of beauty also remain in Adam and Eve ready to be passed down to their ancestors? Could there not also be remnants of the Garden still remaining to cultivate within our souls? Why should the memory of loss, the terror of annihilation, the abandonment of God, the God-trauma remain our only inheritance?

I think, in varying degrees of latency, all of the imbedded visceral memories still echo down from the primordial footprints of Adam and Eve. The seeds of Adam and Eve's earth-life experience stand ready to nurture and empower us, their descendants. The beauties of their first steps in Paradise are their legacy for us to draw from just as much as the sin. Everything depends on what part of their legacy we will choose to draw from. Will we seek the humble path of the Kingdom of God as Jesus taught? Will we know God as our only source and supply of all things good? Or will we persist and perish in the promise of the apple, the lie of the serpent which promised that we too can be like the Most High?

For all of the suffering of human sin birthed by Adam and Eve, so too was the birth of true human dignity and alignment with God. Adam and Eve must have been utterly majestic as they moved in their Garden paradise. All in that world, both inside and around them was completely harmonious, perfectly aligned. Their joy, their dignity, the in-their-bones knowledge of God, was all good. All was the exhilaration of unblemished beauty, all was good, all was God.

We are them, they were ground zero. Adam and Eve's beauty was surpassed only by Jesus in the whole of human history. The first of our kind can be known not just for the shame, but the sublime. Human beings were birthed in beauty, and beauty is our destiny, why not live in it today? Fruits of pleasure and dignity were established into the core of our species and, perhaps, survive waiting to be awakened in us today.

#3 REDEMPTION

We, as Christians, have done "well" in connecting with their sin through our own sin. Could we also still carry the inactivated potential of God-intended greatness? Could we connect with their sublime experience with God through our own capacity to align ourselves with Him? Can we, through Christ and the Holy Spirit in us, make our way back to the Garden? Can we find the pathway to the Kingdom of God within us? Can we make take the path of the prodigal and make our way to the realm of our Father? Can we find a measure of the utter peace, perfected alignment, and the sweet Shalom that Adam and Eve effortlessly walked in? I don't know… but it is a noble quest.

Regardless what one believes about the residual effects of Adam and Eve's lives on our human experience today, there is some usefulness in even metaphorically considering the archetypical themes that we can draw from their story, and how those dynamics can still be playing out today. Their fall from grace is unprecedented, rivaled only perhaps by those angels who rebelled against God. The fall from grace establishes the well-worn path of rebellion, pride and sin which we have all followed, but the story doesn't end there. Ours is the story of paradise lost, and paradise found.

Through faith in Jesus, we are reconciled with God; all that has been lost is and will be restored. We can stand in eternity, inheritance papers in hand, and enter into the perfection of God's creation as it has been His intention from the beginning. Our position, as ones redeemed by the perfection of Jesus' death and resurrection, as citizens of heaven is established. But our sanctified position in Christ is not matched by a joy-dominated condition of joy in this world now. Restored position, yes, restored condition, not yet. I know that I don't access the joy for which I was created to experience. I know the condition of my own heart; I live in fear of life, not in the fullness of life. As I look out at you this morning, I see the strain and fear on your faces as well, and I suspect that we barely scratch the surface of the richness of God's intention.

I know that, because of the curse on this world, because of the broken state in which we live, that we are not able to fully achieve the joy that will one day be given back to us. I know that the sublime experiential unification with God and all things that are His will, will not be accomplished perfectly here on earth, but wouldn't it be kind of fun to try?

We are, perhaps, haunted, by the glory of the past, heights that our species was once afforded. We are sandwiched here on earth in fear and despair, between the forgotten memories of a perfect Garden, and the anticipation of the beauty of Heavenly realms to come. But why not joy now? Why not at least accomplish some of the healing and restoration now that His Kingdom promises? Why not "Thy Kingdom come, Thy will be done," now?

We know paradise lost, but through the experience of heaven we can find paradise-given. When we "Set our sights on the things above, not on the things that are of earth" we can, with God's help, find paradise-realized."

CHAPTER SEVEN

I remember feeling satisfied with how some of this sermon came out. I felt that I was present, in the moment, and that was always satisfying to experience. There were also a number of people who came up to me afterwards with their thoughts and opinions. It seemed as though the sermon was polarizing, stimulating discussions, and I liked that. I was okay, even comfortable, with some conflict, with some debate. Debate gave a precise structure and form which contained in the realm of ideas.

Theories, theology, were familiar playing fields for me to land on, unlike the adrenaline forward roller coaster of Meg. Meg terrified and thrilled me with her spiritual challenges and emotional edge, but I felt that she pushed me too far over the tips of my relational skis and I was comforted to find sanctuary in my sermons. I was also pleased that I could be finding potential intersection points of dreams, and fears and theology.

For that day, I was pleased with my performance, pleased with the direction that all of this was going. I would not stay pleased with myself for very long.

A few nights later, I had what would be the third and final dream. The dream was, like all the dreams, a great comfort and inspiration to me. While the dreams soothed my fears and distress, they also triggered even more thoughts about Meg... thoughts that were anything but soothing.

There was just too much going on between us, at least in my own mind. I felt much more vulnerability than I was comfortable with. Whether intentional or not, she was provocative—pushing me to be more engaged, more alive—but she was also ego crushing in her seemingly low opinion of my abilities. I did not appreciate having my shallowness exposed. I needed to pull back, to find my balance in the sweet silence of detachment. The problem was I now suspected that detachment was a refuge that came with a high price. My emotional numbing was, perhaps, the very state of being which had put such a low ceiling on my spiritual abilities.

Meg was anything but detached and she oozed a Christian muscularity which I was envious of. I desired to be a person who impacted others through his spiritual strength. If impacting others was a value with which I wanted to retain, I needed to have as much grit as grace to get the job done. Meg had the rawness of strength earned that I needed to accomplish to thrive at the work which lay before me.

Regardless of wanting to get in touch with my inner edginess, I'm still cautious at heart. As a way of keeping some emotional distance, I decided to record my dream on a tape recorder. My thought was that, by re-living the dreams directly with Meg too much intimacy was being created. When I spoke the dreams to her, it caused my shields to lower and reveal more of my true self than I was comfortable with, or was healthy to our pastor-to-congregant relationship.

So, I recorded the dream at home and brought it into my office. I felt this was the more professional thing to do. I had even played with the notion, as a power play of sorts, that I would just keep my Heaven dreams to myself. My conscience was pricked by these selfish temptations, so I quickly scratched that plan. I really wanted to do the right kind of things, something befitting my calling.

The roller coaster ride which was my heart, spoke that the truth that the dreams would the best that I could ever offer Meg. There was a certain type of humility which came with the acceptance that it would not be my wisdom, my brilliance, or my character that would be significant to Meg, it would be these dreams. I had to; once again, swallow my pride, my pride which wanted to get credit for any good accomplishment which I stumbled into. I tried to hide my pride, tried to hold it back, but every time I tried to repress it, some of it stuck in my craw refusing to be diminished.

The deplorable truth is that my human heart is so alternately capable of duplicity and then kindness, nobility and then mind-numbing stupidity. At this moment, my heart was saying that Meg deserved the best from me, and I was determined to do my best to live out my heart's good instruction.

On the day of her appointment, Meg walked into my office like a queen. Not a queen in an "entitled princess" kind of way, but rather more of a nobility of presence, someone beautiful to behold. She was at ease and her smile was quick and sincere and whole. We connected through that smile, and I thought, "I'm going to lose her, she will soon be going away," and, in that moment, I was completely at peace with this reality.

She said to me, with her smile warm and sweet, "Every day I listen to the dreams, every day the dreams take me to that place. Every day I am at home. Heaven comes to me, and I want to thank you for it."

She continued, "Years of lost wanderings, every promise made were promises broken. Now… right now, I can see the purpose of every tattered thread. I can say 'Of course, it had to be that way, how could it possibly have been any other way?" I saw the other side of the tapestry; I saw how all things work. Any less pain, any less faith, any person removed from me at the wrong time, would have kept me chained down."

Meg paused; seem to struggle to find her words. Finally, in a voice birthed from every fear and hope which had shaped her life, she looked me in the eyes and said "I also need you to know that I couldn't have done this alone, I needed you here." We sat in silence for a second; we should have sat there like that longer. She showed full evidence of every good hope and prayer which I had directed towards her, but I couldn't just let it be, I couldn't just let it be enjoyed as her special gift which she wanted to share. I had to make this about me.

"You needed me?" I asked. I started thinking of just how well pastoral counseling actually worked, how the combination of a safe place, solid spiritual perspective, and empathy forms a lethal combination of health.

It would turn out that ascribing success to my pastoral counseling skills was just a bit premature.

"Yes, it's just funny how things work," she said.

"What do you mean?" I inquired, as the glow of intimacy faded ever so slightly.

She said, "The key to me seeing behind the tapestry of my life was you. You gave me the pictures, of course, but because you are so uptight, hearing your dreams was like seeing great works of art encased behind glass, something admired but not breathed. Your hyper self-consciousness makes you such an easy target.

"I'm always tempted to mess with you, to mock you and your rigidity, but I needed to practice something different which the dreams awoke in me. I needed to show a kindness towards you that my pride says that you really don't deserve.

"My key in finding life was, in the moment, deciding to accept your weakness and show you some respect anyway. I could have treated you with nothing but my usual disdain. I really just wanted you to feel my pain. The temptation to hurt anyone close to me fuels why I'm mean to you. That's some of the reason that I can be such a pain in the butt. You've heard the old saying that 'it is better that you feel my pain than I do'. I'm not proud of this, but I wanted you, basically a good person, to be shamed like some cruel people had shamed the good in me.

"Treating you kindly required me to act on the kind of faith that I'm rarely able to summons from my soul. I believe in live, yes, but showing grace to others is still an art lost to me. I wanted so badly to diminish you, to make you look the fool. The question was whether I was going to win a battle of my own choosing or surrender to God in this war for love that He fights with me.

"So here is what I did, I remembered the dreams, I surrendered, and the key turned in the lock. It clicked, and I saw my life as it has been. I saw the mechanics of circumstances like thousands of tiny gears in an old fashioned watch. I realize why I judge others so harshly. I also saw that I don't have to be like that"

I was barely even registering anything that she said, "Shame me, and diminish me?" I lashed out. "Come again? You're saying you've been being nice to me, like some kind of pity play? Get over yourself. By the way, if this is you being *nice*, I truly don't want to see your rudeness." I felt myself falling backwards into a great chasm. I had no foothold. I had too quickly awaked from the sweet trance of the Spirit which I had been deeply enjoying.

Grace had departed and I looked for some suitable replacement, some promise of power to push my vulnerability back into the shadows of my own emotional walls. I clutched at the armor of my position and professional image as a way to re-establish some semblance of equilibrium. I slipped these shields over my head like slipping on a sodden, foul smelling sweater. I laughed and said in a voice stronger than I intended, "You have no power over me."

"I do, and we both know it. Now leave it alone" she said. But neither of us could, maybe there was too much poison somehow between us. Maybe the poison just all needed to come out and exact its awful price. "I know that you watch me during your sermons, and I see the way you look at me" she said, warming up to the task. "I know that you hunger for the dust and dirt of the seductive shadow. All that is earth in me wants to diminish you, just to show you. My spirit has soared and now you would crash us both? Our good story is just beginning; don't end it with your foolishness."

I couldn't believe how quickly things had heated up, how quick was the disintegration into darkness. I tried to deny my part in the descent, but her words rang true with alarming clarity, and I was just trying to keep a toehold on the slick slope of panic. I tried to keep some dignity intact, but it was a losing battle.

From the strength of only my pride, I slowly I spat out each word, "I. Don't. Know. What. You're. Talking. About. Try to prove this darkness inside of me, try and you'll see that you're wrong."

"I could prove it to you, but it will cost too much," she replied with an almost casual air.

I smirked a little satisfied smile and that's all it took, she triggered a shadow to come across her eyes that cut me to the core of my being. For a moment, she played me like child batting a balloon in the air, she allowed a moment when she invited lust to fire forward and then shot me down with a look of disgust and pity. The balloon popped and I was shamed and diminished by what had awoken in me for even just that second. What had I done? Why was I so weak?

Reeling from this confrontation, I again try to gather my wits. Instead of quiet and humble, I went loud and proud. I couldn't think, I had lost my mind. "You think too little of me. How dare you think you could play me for the fool. What, you think just because I'm kind to you, you think you own me, you think you could cause me to want you?"

I was offended by my own words; I could only imagine what Meg felt. My words backed me into a corner; I had to play out this farce. I saw her recoil, and I suddenly felt protective of her. She looked like a little girl. I wanted to shield her, to tell her that I was sorry, but I had called down the thunder and now the storm would hit and hit hard.

They say that when a tsunami wave is coming, the ocean seems to suck itself away from the shore. The tide retreats miles out to sea and calls out the song of temptation for people to come, to walk over miles of the ocean floor suddenly exposed. People are fascinated and look to gather the bounty of the sea that they could never have access to otherwise. As people gather fish, and salvage, and wander, the tsunami releases its full power and crashes, sweeps in and destroys. The wave is not intentional with its destruction; it's just the physiology of the dynamics unleashed.

Meg's recoil, her vulnerability, pulled me to her. Then she crashed on me with her words and ways. "I told you not to play this game." Her voice was harsh and cold, but her eyes danced again with the hint of a thousand wanton promises. I was simultaneously stunned and inflamed. How could someone transform so quickly, she was moving as a shadow cast by fast-moving clouds. Her words shifted to match the soft dance of her eyes. "I could make you break any vow that you've ever held sacred." This might have been meant to be insulting, but I could only feel the want and opportunity of promise fulfilled.

Her words turned sharp again. "Is this what you want, pastor, is this who you are?" All I could hear was the dialectic of her seducing eyes that said, "This is who you are, stop pretending... besides, who will ever know?"

I reached my hand forward, only wanting to stroke back a wisp of her tussled hair. She spat in my face. Disgusted, I flung myself away from her, but before I could wipe the spit from my face her fingers were pressed firmly on my eyelids. "Keep your eyes closed, blind man." Her voice came from the depths reserved for either the insane or for the prophet.

Still not free from my own chains of want, I kept my eyes closed and waited. She seemed to walk slowly to the far side of the room and back. She spit again violently in my face and then gently wiped it off with the office tissues which I keep only for tears.

"Now you can see what there is to see."

Her voice shook me to the core. I opened my eyes to a filtering of light and dark. Light and dark passed back and forth, like a physical force from her, in her, and around her. I gasped out loud as I saw the same shadows of light and dark colliding through me and around me. Light and dark were in a deadly battle within me. My heart was the battlefield and a prize would go to the victor. I despaired in thought, I despaired in my being. The dark night of my soul was playing itself out in broad daylight.

I slammed my eyes shut again and screamed in my heart for forgiveness, for deliverance. I stumbled to my desk as if drunk and willed the shaking of my hand to stop long enough to press "play" on the tape recorder. After a complex tug of war between all that was dark and light, it was the soft and simple which would rescue us, a simple clear note of sanity from beyond. The sound that I heard was my own voice, again, telling the narrative of my latest dream. Together, Meg and I listen to my dream of a heavenly traveler.

In that moment, I didn't hear the dream story as a creative accomplishment or personal achievement. I knew then that I could never see it as a vehicle to fame, a gratification of my ego. I heard the dream for what it was: a healing, a sanctuary, a treatment for the diseases of flesh and spirit that controlled me in the moment. It was a mother's soft voice, a father's strong heart. If there was such a thing as good shame, I felt that in full measure. I heard again of the woman and the tapestry and the beauty... and serenity was restored.

As the dream story ended for that day, as the tape stopped playing, I hesitantly looked in Meg's direction, afraid of what I'd see, afraid of what I'd feel.

Meg had again been transformed in the telling of the dream. We looked again at each other, searching for some vestige of the sweet respect and connection which we had enjoyed earlier that day. It seemed we were both surprised that she could even tolerate my presence. Finding a measure of grace shared again, she mumbled, "I'll see you next time," and we stumbled away from each other, unnerved and uncertain, and each of us more than a bit disgusted at my behavior.

She paused at the door. "This was the trauma of Adam and Eve; you felt the abandonment caused by their betrayal. This is what they saw and felt, the knowledge of good and evil. How'd you like it?"

After she left, I sobbed for hours. My nose would not stop running; I had been physically, emotionally, spiritually turned inside out. Some years later, I would tell someone that this was the one time that I was certain that I'd heard God's voice. It was the physicality of the whole thing, which felt real, my body seemed to groan and creak like a frozen pipe about to burst. I waited for an explosion which, thankfully, never came.

I had always thought that for humans to even slightly touch upon the actual presence of God would be wildly disconcerting, and for me, it was. How can we, being the broken, confused, imperfect beings that we are, hold our stuff together in the presence of such purity? I don't know, I just know that I didn't.

So, God had spoken to me then, the problem was that he didn't seem particularly happy with me, His flawed vessel. Yet, it was His beauty which kept me sane. It was the joy of His sweet gift which took my breath away and allowed me to catch again the rhythm of joy and hope. I played the recording of the dream again and again. I hung onto it like the life preserver it was. This is what I heard, just what I needed, just in the nick of time.

CHAPTER EIGHT

The garden was familiar to her even though she had no conscious memory of it. There was no garden like this in her earth-life experience. She was pulling from a memory that she had no context for. Whether it predated earth-life, she could not say.

She could see the garden's outline in her mind; she knew it like she knew her private thoughts. This garden was intensely personal to her; she knew instinctively what it needed from her, and what she needed from it. As she walked deeper into it, she slightly recoiled as she realized just how sensitized that she was to each aspect of this place. She felt a power awaken within her, and then a giving power released outward from her.

She noticed that wherever she glanced, the plants drew nourishment from her. She could see the foliage of the leaves come to life. The garden was drinking her in like she was water, food, and sunlight—all in one. She relaxed and started to chuckle as she saw flowers come to bloom at her touch. She walked, she saw, she healed. The garden was her garden. She delighted at the beauty which was given to this place simply by her good intention, simply by the openness of her heart to good, simply by her faith that she could give birth to beauty.

The dwelling where she had been deposited as she transitioned from life to life, the place of the cliffs where her tapestry hung, this was still home to her. The home of the cliffs was where she knew she would return to at the end of this day. She belonged there; but this garden spoke home to her in an even deeper sense. Her garden here was a place where she could see herself—past, present, and future. Everything made sense; everything here resonated in and through her.

The garden became more and more alive as she walked through it. It was breathing, it was expanding, it was singing. She began to see that it represented all the good that had ever been done to her and for her. The good in her life, whether it be her past, present or future good, was all concentrated here.

She had been the one who had opened her heart to good by the opening of that door, but now good was coming alive in her and around her. Like the frozen ground of winter becoming alive as the last vestiges of snow melts away, the truth of good was being born in her and now it was her turn to soak it all up.

The garden was a personal place, the garden was an eternal place, and the garden was a Jesus place. Jesus the Incarnate, His presence is strong here. Jesus, God-man, the first of a new order of beings. Jesus, who stood at the intersection of divine and human. Jesus, the personification of redemption and birth. Jesus, the One she had known so little about prior to her passing.

As she walked the garden, the woman watched as scenes from her past begin to play out before her eyes. There was no threat from anything she saw. She was coming to know that this was an especially holy place for her. She'd seen the other side of the tapestry; she'd witnessed scenes of goodness each living moment of her new life. Now she watched as unseen hands had presented gifts of blessings on a platter to her throughout her earth-life.

She had thought, prior to her passing, that she was the master of her life, that whatever good she'd experienced was gained by the sweat of her brow and the labor of her hands. Now she was shown threads of connections, literal golden strands of purpose and power, which had been invisible gifts provided to her. She saw the invisible protectors who were there for her at precisely the right time in her earth-life to keep darkness at bay.

She saw the rightness in times when her protectors lingered and did not intervene, when they gave her space, just like the old caretaker had to make her own choices. The traveler could see back then that these protectors had given her a prompting in her heart to seek them, to talk to them. But her heart had been cold and afraid in her earth-state and she was unable to respond.

She saw that her protectors then, much like her garden now, did not begrudge her the right to her blindness, the right to harden her heart towards them, God, and life. There was no judgment here, only healing, health and wholeness. She knew that all was unfolding at its own pace, and in its perfect time. So, it was not especially painful for her to watch scenes of what she would have previously called her failings and her foolishness.

She saw ways that she had not even approached the best of her capabilities, and she saw the hurt to her own spirit and the hurtfulness towards others caused by her actions and attitudes and words. She saw the gravity of what fear and pride and cruelty could do. She stood still and silent and allowed herself to add the overflowing ingredient of relentless love to the sadness which theses earth-life scenes revealed. She was humbled, but not shamed. Sadness and shame had once defined her, but no more.

She gave love generously to any barrenness in her own soul, just as she generously gave love to the garden blooming around her. Tears didn't exist in this heaven and she felt heaven's grace in full measure. She soaked it all in for an unmeasurable amount of time. It was the voice of the garden which finally shook her out of her reverie.

The garden sang, the garden whispered, "Oh, for so long we have desired this day for you, this day for us. Long have we watched, dormant and mute, waiting for you to sing your healing into being. How good is He who gives you the skills to garden. Now come follow your path, in this, your place, to your greatest joy."

The woman walked on the path and saw something shaped like an old-fashioned well, the kind that medieval villagers would have drawn water from long ago. It's made of cobblestone and it was of perfect height for her to look down into without effort or strain. There was water in the well, but it was more of a thick, golden liquid, than something slippery and thin. The water did not reflect, it had a different purpose, the water did not reflect, it revealed.

The woman saw the people of her heart in the depths of the water. She saw her family: her parents, her husband, her children, her brother, and sisters. They are there; this was not like a dream but more like a portal to see reality as it truly is. They look at her with smiling faces, strong, perfect, and engaged.

Her loved ones looked better than she could have ever imagined or hoped for. They continued to come into focus as their images came to the surface. Her family is now before her in perfect clarity, and they begin to speak. They spoke to her from their hearts, they spoke to her words that only she would know. At this, the woman cried. She cried from a place where she was so profoundly moved, so deeply touched.

She sobbed from the pure release of tension in her heart. They were all beautiful, they were all young, and they were so at ease, so at peace, so thrilled to see her. They looked at her with pure wisdom and compassion in their eyes and hearts. They had become, and now were, everything they were meant to be. They were whole, they were joyful, and they were safe. They were dignified, they were restored, they were noble. They were alive, they were so alive, and they were beautiful.

DR. MONTE PRIES | Chapter Eight

They told her of how, at her passing, she kept repeating "Jesus, Jesus" which surprised them greatly and impacted their lives even more. They were grateful to Him. Her loved ones story of her passing triggers for the woman the glimpse of a memory of a door, and a Light, and the person of Jesus partially revealed. The traveler smiles from the depths of her gratitude.

Not for the first time, the woman released a deep breath that she had no idea she was holding back. She could not take her eyes away from the wonder before her. She was filled with indescribable joy and satisfaction. She could gaze into their enlightened eyes forever, receiving from these, her loved ones, the full measure of their own unique beauty and goodness. They laughed, they laughed, and they all laughed some more. They could not get over how truly good things were, and how truly great God is. The gratitude shared between them was like a physical force bubbling up and spilling over this seeing-well.

They shared, just with their eyes, all of the need for forgiveness, asked for and received. After endless joy passed back and forth, they look at her once more as a way to say, "goodbye, but not for long." They looked at her and their eyes were kind and twinkling with a secret. A secret which suggested that there was still so much good to be revealed. Their eyes spoke as they were leaving, and their leaving created a space for something equally satisfying to be revealed in the sacred waters.

The waters stirred and her family was gone, but their laughter and wisdom were so strong in her heart that she would never again to be without their beauty and their presence. In this extraordinary way, her deepest wishes have come true. She had never even allowed herself to think such things, and yet, here were the longings of her unknown soul, come to the surface to be lived out and fulfilled.

She noticed, after a while, that the waters were beginning to calm and become clear again. She was curious as she looked again into their depths. A new face appeared in the reflection and it literally took her breath away. It was her own reflection in the water; it was her eyes which she now stared into. She felt stunned. She saw herself. This was not a reflection of someone who might be, or something that once was, this was her, this was now, and it was so good. The face looking back showed an elevation of being; a depth of character that she fully recognized as her own, and yet, felt utterly amazed by. She had been increasingly less shocked by the manifestations of true life around, but now she was amazed by the true life within her.

Her experience in this world, this place of cleansing, healing, and the power of beauty, has worked the deepest kind of good magic. It is her, fully realized, firing on all cylinders of body, mind, and spirit to a degree that she could never have thought possible. She was awake, she was alive, she was real, and the person who looked back at her, was all that she could have ever hoped to be, and then some.

She felt the right kind of pride. All was right, everything works together, all has been made new. This was there for her all along, it had always been there for her to discover. She looked into the well of water and saw scenes from the life that she once knew. She saw again her life story of sadness and hurt. An image of pain was there, but only for a second, replaced by the same scene as it was meant to be played out, but for the brokenness of the previous world, and her previous self. Perfection and joy had been unleashed to absorb every aspect of her past life. Perfection and joy now free to reclaim the whole of her life and make her life their own. Life and life's circumstances were making amends to her—and she with it.

As the redemption scenes played out before her in the pool of water, so did the scenes continue to play out in her heart, mind and soul. The shadows of pain in her life were juxtaposed alongside of scenes of beauty and healing. She was seeing her life now through the redeeming eyes of God. She viewed scenes from the heart of God and experienced all of the beauty that would have been hers to know sooner, had the world not been cursed by Adam's fall.

What the dream-traveler had known to be her past had been re-cast and the shadows in her life replaced by light. She *experienced the whole of her life as it had been intended it to be and she took her time digesting all of the good that was being hard-driven into her. Opportunities never realized on earth were brought to life. This, her life script redeemed, wrote out these new realities.*

Things forgotten, sweet moments remembered, all were being woven into a new tapestry of identity and reality. This was the good-life script, a story predetermined and yet never brought into being, but now it shone. Shadows continued to fade as a new dawn continued to rise, again and again, page after sacred page.

She was completely at ease. She was free to move, to think, to act. She realized why she had been so afraid in what she used to call life. She was afraid, in part, because she was operating so far beneath the capacity that she now felt. Up until her so-called "death," she had been ill-prepared to succeed. She half suspected that something on earth was wrong all along, that things were not the way they were supposed to be, but she had no way at the time of even finding the words to express these fragments of feelings.

In her old life, somewhere, something had been demanding her to be more, to be someone that she could never come close to being by her willpower alone. She remembers realizing how broken she was in her earth-life; but she could never get close to finding what she needed to fix herself. She had tried; she was just not up to the task of winning at life with the cards she had been dealt.

She also knew that feeling oneself to be ill-equipped to succeed in earth-life was a curse, to differing degrees, for all of her species. The brokenness of the human race was something which nobody and nothing on earth was exempt from.

She knew now that she could not fix herself on earth any more than she was fixing herself now. She was being advanced, being restored—not through her efforts, but by the sublime quality of the place where she now resided. Her heightened character was not the result of willpower, but rather an outgrowth of the beauty of the place. She loved the whole of this world, but she loved this garden most of all.

Her companions had not come into the garden, they were somewhere else. But the garden had taken up the companion role. The garden loved her, spoke softly to her like a mother, played endlessly with her like a friend, and came up to her like a treasured pet excited to see her when she returned home at the end of the day. The garden was connected to her—to her thoughts, prayers, and dreams. She was there forever, but like every aspect of her journey, a relentless hunger to know more awoke her curiosity to see what was next to come.

The garden's eyes were upon her and it directed her path as she walked deeper into its soul. The garden never did begrudge the woman in her desire to find new paths of wonder. The garden guided her along the banks of a tumbling brook in a forest of autumn leaves. A sun-drenched clearing in the trees drew her attention. All was golden in the forest—the leaves, the light, the sparkle in the water—but there was something especially bright and shiny in this clearing. There was a golden staircase ascending upwards, towards the sky.

Some things are golden on the surface, like a pretty veneer which can become chipped or be scraped away. This staircase was different than that; it was golden from within, a living and breathing vessel of gold. She hesitated at the foot of the staircase.

She had been in her garden; she had been in this new world…for what seemed like forever. Even from the beginning, from when she first slid into this heaven, things felt somehow familiar to her. The staircase was different though, it felt otherworldly to her. She suspected that, if she walked up, she would come down the staircase a much different person.

Despite her hesitation, she wasn't afraid; all it took was a friendly breeze from the garden moving her in the direction of the staircase. The breeze was just the little nudge that she needed to walk up the stairs. She started to climb, but soon the stairs simply elevated her to a place just above the clouds. She *stepped off of the golden stairs and onto a platform, which has partially pierced the ceiling of the cloud cover. She could look down and see her feet still firmly planted on the platform. The rest of her body, mind, and spirit was above the clouds, now in a different place altogether.*

What she saw above the clouds was the vast unfurling depth and dimension of eternity. It was quiet, still and timeless. Since leaving earth, each space seemed even more serene that the space before. Each dimension crossed was opening up with deepening degrees of wordless clarity.

Orientating herself to this new space, the woman could not get over just how quiet, just how still all things were around her. The tangible force of deep stillness had a profound impact on her. The woman had never thought to consider that there could be varying degrees of quiet and stillness, just like there are depths and dimensions of subtle shifts in color. In her earth-life, quiet and stillness were experienced as one-dimensional, there was either quiet, or not quiet. This was something different all together.

In the space above the clouds, quiet entered into the dream traveler being as a deeper dimension than the woman could ever have imagined. The quiet here was not just quiet in an "absence of sound" kind of way, it was that, but the presence of quiet was the domineering essence, a kaleidoscope of silence.

She felt more than slightly unnerved by the differentness of this place. For the comfort of the familiar, she continued to look down at her feet, which were still standing in a place that made sense to her, the reality below. She wanted to feel the weight of her grounded-ness before the exploration of something so new and different. She breathed, she remembered her God, she remembered her companions, she saw her garden in her heart, and she knew all was good, all was safe. Sufficiently restored, she looked at the wonder before her.

Countless different eternal dimensions presented themselves for her inspection. She felt like a patron in a high-end restaurant, where there were pages and pages of dining options from which to choose. She had been elevated to a place where all of history drifted before her like a New Year's Day parade on display. Her feet were still grounded, but she floated through the galaxies of time and place, spaces of profound truth and beauty.

She drifted on. All of history moved before her and with her. There was nothing big, there was nothing small, it all just passed in a wonderfully neutral way before her. If she was still confined to earth-life, she might have said that "she was taking her time, taking it all in." The truth was that time, once again, was one thing that was not there for her taking. She felt the quality of the eternal ever since she has left earth, yet for her the absence of time is even more pronounced in this place. There is nothing here but the eternal now.

Time was not present, but God certainly was. His Presence was achingly personal and powerful. The woman knew that she was in the deeper realm of God. She gazed out into the place of purity, a place where she could see pure beauty, and the knowledge which underlays all of existence. She saw that eternity and eternal truths were the ever-present canvas on which God painted. She saw that the life that was governed by time received only the reflection of the pure works of God's hands.

What she saw here was pure life, and in perfect silence, truths and beauty rolled out in front of her like waves stretching over a forever ocean. Each wave is perfect in its own right, and each more perfect than the last. None of these waves of truth and beauty were either small or large; they were just each exquisitely formed by the hands and dreams of God.

She became intoxicated by the pure. She longed to follow each wave. She wanted to let go and become formless, to be a wisp of moisture above the wave, carried by its momentum to nothingness. She let this desire pass, like all things were passing before her. No reaction, no want, just acceptance. Before her all things move, and they move without judgement from her and without judgment towards her. She just is, and she stayed like this forever.

When she does take any account of things, she struggles to remember even where she is and who she is. She takes stock of her position and condition on this journey. She looks away from the parade of scenes on display and she cautiously looks down.

Other than her feet, which she could still see standing on the platform; she had become stretched thin, ethereal like the most delicate of fibers in paper, weightless and translucent, barely held together. Light shined through her and from her, she was not of enough physical substance to even create a shadow. Something about this place was reconstructing her into a never before realized purity, and she loved it.

The reflected image of herself that she's seen in the garden, the image of herself which had so delighted her, the picture of herself serene and noble, even now that seemed in comparison to be an unnecessary weight to carry. It suddenly meant nothing for her to only dispassionately observe all things; she began to yearn to join all things, to be merged into the everything and the nothing of being. The siren's call to become absorbed into ecstasy and beauty threatened to lift her off the platform and into a formless embrace.

But at that point, without ever turning around, the woman sensed that she was not alone. A presence had joined her on the platform above the clouds. There was a gentle hand on her shoulder. The hand was kind, comforting, light and strong. The presence there was one who spoke to her of how right it was for her to yearn for the wonder of being swallowed up forever in the ecstasy of all things good.

The presence there with her was one well-acquainted with the perfection of this place, and of the traveler's growing hunger to be there, to stay there. The woman felt the presence lovingly directing her to begin to return to her journey. She felt the invitation to return to the garden, to rejoin her companions, to seek the fullness of wisdom available ahead of her.

The woman began to feel that the presence here with her was actually a future manifestation of herself, someone who she would eventually become. The woman is told to think of herself as a hummingbird that, for now, lands softly, lightly, on many good places. The presence speaks of herself as one who has learned to come to this place to draw its sweetness, like a hummingbird drawing nectar from a flower. A hummingbird which is good at drawing out sweetness, and knowing what to receive, but then knowing also when to leave. The woman feels the rightness in how she is being directed, and fully submits to the rhythm of her travels.

It was no accident that the woman was getting help here with her desires, and she felt grateful. The woman knew that she lacked the wisdom to endlessly drink in the purity of this place. She also knew that she had been altered and she would never be the same. She would journey far and wide to gain whatever she needed to return, again, to this place. The heaven traveler was confident that when she returned to this realm of the purely eternal, she would possess the necessary wisdom to make full use of all of its wonder. She reflects now on how she will get back to her journey; she is not anxious, only curious, ready to learn.

The touch of the presence on her shoulder further oriented the woman back to the world of the garden. The touch on the shoulder assured her, again, that this was right for her to see, but that it was not the right place for her to join... at least not now. Slowly, ever so gently, she began to separate from the true eternal. Still light as a feather, now barely visible in the garden world, she began to descend back to the garden.

The woman landed as soft as a beam of moonlight on the garden floor. She was more light shadow than solid, but she knew that she had forever to regain the form she had before she ascended those golden stairs. The garden itself was a place reverberating with quiet and peace, strongly seasoned by the power of the Eternal. The garden, her garden, was a good place to just be and acclimate, to transition back from the experience of seeing Eternity in all of its purity and essence.

Being grounded again in the physical realm, the woman slowly re-acquired her physical form. She had been drifting with the flow of the garden, carried on its breeze. She is content to float on the garden's breath, trusting in the goodness which guides her.

As she begins to find again the power of her own will, as she begins to regain the divinely given gift of intention, she finds that she can will herself to head in directions of her own choosing. She is silently invited to go back to the world she was in before the garden, back to the world of the tapestry, the lions, the angels, and the quiet, serene man. She accepted the invitation to return to this realm and she moved towards a gate which she determined to be the back entrance to her garden.

Still dazed and deeply moved, she stumbled through the gate and right into the strong arms of a waiting angel. Now outside of her garden, the woman becomes more aware of the effects which the realm above the clouds had on her physical being. She is still translucent. There was barely enough tangible material of the woman for the angel to contain, but the angel scooped up what was left of her and placed her onto the back of the largest lion. The angel then wrapped her in a light, shiny cocoon-like fabric, which allowed for the woman to have enough substantial form to function in this world. She was safe and secure on the lion's back as the companions came together again into their "journey formation" and walked away from the gate of the garden.

When she was drifting in the Eternal, watching all of truth, wisdom, love, and history pass before her, her physical body had become more like a granular ash than flesh and bone. The one physical piece that had retained its form were her eyes which had remained fully intact. In fact, she had felt, and continued to feel as if she was all eye. She had no real tangible connection with the rest of her body in this present form, but she felt that her eyes had been burned by the purity of the most heavenly realm. Burned, not in a tragic way, but more burned like a refining fire would burn with purity and purpose.

Her eyes were alive, and even now they sparkled with power and wisdom. The power that comes from detachment,

detachment from dependency on the circumstances of life, and the wisdom that comes from seeing things that are most real. She could feel her eyes piercing power to discern and disarm. Again she is struck by the paradox of strength gained through the quiet art of detachment, the gentle path of acceptance.

Wrapped in the cocoon of shimmering power, she was, once again, at the mercy of her love designated companions. There is a wonderful comfort in being carried by these devoted ones whose singular focus was to fling her forward in her journey. Her eyes could see, her eyes pierced through any obstacle; and yet she was like a baby in her mother's arms as the lion moved forward with its stately strides.

CHAPTER NINE

*T*he gate had opened to the sweet light of a quiet beach. It was the beach that the woman remembered seeing from the dwelling where she had first woken in this new world. The beach was dreamy and soft, a perfect re-introduction to this world.

The world was everything that she had remembered it to be. It was safe, alive, healthy, and whole. She was so grateful and she praised God with a heavenly voice—a voice which she realized must have been acquired in the eternal realm. The five companions: the two lions, the two angels, and the wise man all smiled as they knew the places she had been, and they delighted in the pleasure which they knew the dream traveler must be feeling.

As they traveled forward, the woman began to hear sound again. She picked up the soft and padded swishing sound that the lions made as they walked on the sand. She could hear of the rippling of small waves and the tumbling of sea shells and sands as the waves chased onto the shore. The call of a seagull drifted on the breeze.

The sun was kind and sweet, and once again the woman noticed that it filled and nourished her, there was no harshness to its touch. The salt air was sweet and tangy, it fully awakened her senses. She gazed out at the clear waves forming windows to view the colors of the ocean floor. She continues to be content to ride, to be in the loving embrace of her companions. She again felt the sacredness of their perfect intentions for her, she was the object of their complete attention, and she knew their pride in being a part of what was being so successfully accomplished in her.

A wide berth of soft white sand began to narrow as the group rounded a point of land that jutted out into the sea. She noticed again the dwelling in the cliff, the home where she'd first arrived, or as the woman was now thinking, the house where she had been born. There was a river, the "laughing river" which she had so enjoyed when she was first adjusting to her eternal life. The river was emptying itself into the sparkling seas, and there is some still undefinable quality of this river which made her smile once again.

The woman, or I should say, the lions turned inland, towards the lake by her "born-again" home. The area around the lake was cool and clear and freshly scented by rain that had fallen on pine needles warmed by the sun. The woman was still so altered, so light of heart and in physical substance. What was left of her physical being was placed on the lake's water and she drifted off. Her companions waited patiently at the shoreline. There was no hurry in the woman, or in her companions. The companions were attentive, at peace, and they give the feeling that they had each done this before, many times.

As the woman drifted, the water took on a transformative effect. She was being altered in a similar way as she had been altered in the pool by her tapestry inside her dwelling in the cliffs. In fact, the water that was in her pool was the same water that had run down into the lake. It was living water, having the power to cleanse, unburden—or in this case—restore a solid physical form to its being. Similar to when she had first soaked in the pool in her house above, she felt a soft tingling sensation, an energy slowly massaging her into a solid form.

As the massaging did its work, her physical form became solid enough to allow her to slip under the surface of the lake. She sank slowly down into the depths until she finally landed on the sandy bottom. There was still enough light to see the white clouds above the cool waters. She noticed that, underneath the water, beautiful colors were everywhere. The colorful fish left a trail of spectacularly colorful bubbles as they darted about.

The woman was fully free to simply sit, and watch, and think. There was no deadline pressing her, whatsoever. She had nothing to build, nothing to protect, and nothing to solve. Her physical form was gradually returning to her, but she still carried with her the eyes of the eternal, the eyes that simply watched and waited. She felt the light of her eternal eyes acclimating to the physicality of the world around her and within her. She accepted of all what has happened and was happening, and she accepted it all with gratitude.

She loved being in the depths of the lake. She loved that, with the notable exception of her eyes, all her senses were muted under the water. This muted quality of sound and taste, touch, and feel reminded her of the eternal place in the garden. Except for the fact that the water was transforming her into her physical form (in contrast to the eternal place which took away her physicality), being in the depths of the lake allowed her to simply observe life without response, comment, or attachment. She was free to think, she was free to be detached, and quiet, and still.

Each step of the journey has had its place and purpose. The wonder of each experience was exhilarating and satisfying. Each experience was an elevation, a deepening of her being. She had no regrets, she was in no rush. Seasons passed, days drifted, and still she sat on the bottom of the lake, lost in contemplation.

She was still suspended between worlds, not wanting to simply shake off the effects of the eternal on her body, mind and spirit—it was too good, and it was too pure to simply be set aside. So, she rested in the depths of silence and allowed the *water to do its work, and she allowed the strong, tender arms of quiet to integrate the different lessons of her journey within her heart, soul, and mind.*

Then she began to rise. Like an air bubble making its way to the surface, she moved towards the release that came as water touched air. She was ready, so she allowed herself to drift from the sweet embrace of the deep. The sun, the warmth, with each passing phase of rising, the breath of life and air called her to the surface. Higher and higher she effortlessly rose, until she broke the surface of the calm. She, again, was set to drift on the surface of the lake, but this time not as a wisp, but as a woman restored.

She intentionally allowed herself nothing to do but to float on her back, to see the soft blue sky, to feel the warm, to watch the passing clouds and hear the songs of a dozen birds. She was safe, she was happy; she smiled as she washed up on the shore like a sweet forgotten memory brought to life.

Her body was new, born again to be born-again; she was solid, strong, and light. Standing now on the sandy shore, knee-deep still in water, she looked at the mirror reflection of the calm lake. She was curious to see what the lake's surface might reflect. She looked down and saw the face that she'd seen in the reflecting well in the garden. Her face was the same—with one notable exception, one significant alteration. Her eyes were ablaze with light, they were filled with passion, wisdom, and special sight. Her eyes gleamed, intense and powerful and kind. The eternal in her has come fully alive and will never be lost.

It was those eyes which bore into me then as I looked on with breathless wonder. Her eyes were piercing, pleading... passionate circles of light. Then the dream traveler spoke to me, and any breath which remained in my chest rushed out with the push of fresh adrenalin.

"I am not the same woman who spoke with you before. The energies of heaven drift in, around, and through me and I am different. I feel like I have less to say, but more to give. You have seen what has happened on my journey.

You have seen events unfold, but nothing can describe just how wonderful it all is. Wonderful... full of wonder, that says it the best. I live in a perpetual state of wonder and it's intoxicating and completely satisfying.

"I wish that you could know now what your own special place will be like. I know that all of this will become true for you. You will be elevated, you will be dignified, you will know delight. This place, your place... heaven waits for you. Heaven holds its breath until you are here, and then it moves with you, sings with you, journeys with you.

"Forever is your best friend. Knowing God, in eternity, is your greatest joy. Work your heart and your imagination around what I say. Dream these things, practice these truths. Practice knowing the great truth, which is that you don't die, you never die. I'll say this again, because different people hear things differently at different times, "YOU DON'T DIE." Your body dies so that you can move into forever. You are not your body, you will know this soon. You are spirit, soul, heart, and mind, that is you and you never end.

"Think of what I am saying in this way, your body exists as a house for your spirit, soul, heart, and mind. If your home on earth, the roof over your head, if this place on earth burned to the ground, you would not cease to exist. You might be sad, maybe even devastated for a bit, but you would do what people do, you would move on. So it is when your body crumbles and collapses under all the weight it bears, you move on. You move on, you move on. You move on with less fuss and bother than when someone loses the roof over their head on earth.

"At some point, you will come to know the white, the quiet, the stillness of the pure eternal. You will dispassionately gaze upon all that is. You will see and know the depths and dimensions of God's creation and have a glimpse into His very being. Even now, the thought of this, the truth of this, makes me smile. I hope that I can gaze upon your joy when you are brought there. Perhaps I can. You and I are linked, you know. I felt the loving eyes of others when all of existence paraded before my eyes, when my eyes first burned with beauty and discernment. I was surrounded by many. I could feel their comforting gaze. Maybe I will see you there; maybe I will be chosen to give comfort to you at just the right time.

"I find that words are a labor for me right now. Forgive me. I have a feeling that I won't stay long in the afterglow of this ecstasy. I know we both have tasks left to accomplish, but for now, join me in quiet. Close your eyes and imagine that you are joining me, that you are embraced by the beauty which God has visited upon me. Imagine yourself completely secure. Feel your companions around you. Imagine them looking at you with pleasure, their very faces pathways for the Lord's love to travel. Sit with me on the warm sands of this still lake. Breathe in the scent of pine and ocean breeze as soft winds ripple the still calm of the lake's water. All is well, God is good."

Still in the dream, I allow myself to join her in her quiet. I knew that I was asleep, yet I had never felt more awake. Her serenity is like a physical force stretching across space and time. She is charismatic in her stillness, she is contagious. I have never experienced anything approaching this level of well-ness. I am not pastor, I am not father, I am not fool, I simply am. I am like this for what feels like forever. I smile. My trance of joy ends with the sound of her sweet voice.

"I am only allowed to share a portion of beauty with you. There are reasons why you are there and I am here, but all will come to pass in due season. Forgive me; talking requires effort right now, an effort that I don't want to sustain. We will talk again, but not now. I must go. Let's see what happens next. Pay attention"

As I caught my breath after the heart-stopping intensity of those eyes, and the purity of peace in my soul, the dream shifted back to the unfolding story.

DR. MONTE PRIES | Chapter Nine

The woman and her companions were there at the water's edge, they stood on the half-moon spread of sand. When she caught the eye of the largest lion, her attention was directed towards the back end of the sandy beach and a fluttering of wonder color. There sat a majestic tent. The tent's half-open flaps are swaying in the wind they offer her an invitation. The rippling movement of cloth, the rhythm of breezes, and the sweet breath of life flowed in and around this pavilion. The word "wisdom" seemed to be drifting on the wind.

The energy here, the aura of knowledge made her curious and curiosity pulled her towards the tent. She lifted back the flaps of the entrance and stepped inside.

The space inside was impossibly vast. Not for the first time, she was taken back by alterations of space and time not available to her in her previous world. The ceiling of the big top pavilion was like the roof of space itself. She saw planets circling by, and clouds of color and light. She brought her focus down to three women, who reached out to greet her. They have a similar physical demeanor to the man of serenity who has acted as her silent companion. The women differed though, in the way in which they moved and in the intense sparkle of their eyes. The serene man's eyes were a warm glow of amber brown, these women's eyes radiated with the impossibly blue light of electricity. They were smiling eyes, birthed of a thousand peals of laughter.

The three women of the tent motioned for the traveler to sit down, so sit down she did. They immediately launched into teachings of the deepest kind of wisdom. They taught with passion, clarity, and most of all, humor. They were enlightened, entertaining, and hilarious teachers. She sat, mesmerized by their depth of knowledge, and the sharp, incisive quality of their comic genius. The woman laughed, non-stop forever, as the insights of the ages were downloaded into her being.

Each convulsion of hilarity opened up even more fully the very pores of her heart, soul, and mind. Knowledge had always

115

been tedious to her, she had struggled and resisted it, but now her eyes have been opened.

The foundational rationale underlying the power of all spiritual things was being given to her. Despite needing no further proof of God's existence and perfect nature, she was given revelation. Each small piece of the foundation opened the door to more understanding and even greater joy.

When she was on earth, until the very end of life there, she had not been much of a believer in spiritual things; she had thought she needed proof in order to believe. Now that she has embraced the truth that it is her spiritual side which is her dominate life force, she did not need any more proof of God's existence other than the beauty around her.

Before she had "died," she believed that she needed all of her questions answered and explained before she would believe in God. Now all things were explained. She thought it ironic that while she found the exercise to be delightful, facts were not her pathway to God, beauty was. That is not to say that she wasn't immensely enjoying the intellectual power which the women brought to the table.

What the three women taught her about the true nature of things was deep, wild, and wonderful. She was utterly fascinated; all brain cells available to her were firing at high speed, and the fact that her teachers made her laugh so hard just enabled the truths to plunge deep into her core.

As much as she had always enjoyed laughter, she had not been fully aware of laughter's capacity to bear her soul to the message connected to it. Once again, she opens up; breathing, relaxing, and allowing good life, God life, full access to her being. Once again, the traveler further lowered the shields around her heart, shields that she had no idea still existed.

The woman had thought that she had fully released all resistances to heaven's grace; she was surprised to see otherwise. When she commented to her teachers that she was still holding part of herself back, one of the women said, "Oh yeah, you are still wound tighter than a drum." That teacher immediately started using the traveler's head as a bongo drum. The teacher played out a highly sophisticated rhythm on the woman's head, a beat that seemed to have a language all its own, but to the woman's ears the beat spoke clearly. The woman heard as clearly as if the bongo beat was speaking words in her own native tongue. It was all so funny to her. The woman couldn't believe that one of these profound teachers was actually using her head as an instrument, pounding out this beautiful teaching in such a wonderfully absurd way.

The woman can't stop laughing at the ridiculousness of having her head drummed on. She is not embarrassed in any way, it's just so funny. It felt so good to laugh. Another layer of joy is how her teachers revealed complex truths to her in such a simple way. In the face of irrefutable logic, all she could do was to laugh and say, "Of course, how could I have not seen that before?" The four of them laughed and laughed, their joy took on a life form all its own. It was so freeing to the dream traveler, she couldn't stop herself, she can't hold back. She was naked before them, she is open and free. Her laughter is like a fresh rush of wind sweeping away any remnants of stale thoughts and toxic memories.

Silly and sweet, poignant and brilliant, the teaching, the laughter continued, and it rolled on and on. The pleasure in this was more than the woman could ever have believed to be possible. How could the simple act of laughter extend her so far, and raise her so high? In all of the wonders that the woman has seen, somehow this time of laughter with these women catches her most off guard. Laughter has become a physical force inside of her, like a living organ that has been transplanted within her. She can't shake the giggles and she wouldn't want to even if she could.

She felt so much gratitude to her teachers, there is such a bond between them. She saw the brilliance of their minds, she has been undone by the brilliance of their humor, and yet she knew that they were just as "serious" about their task as her protective company of companions were of theirs.

Finally, after another forever sequence of thinking, breathing, and intoxicating laughter, the woman started becoming aware of a shift of energies within her. She felt so pumped up, like the light of her being was fully on and her spiritual motor running just for the thrill of feeling its own power. She began to feel a little restless and started looking around and wondering about the world outside of the pavilion. She wanted to run, fly, play, and learn. She looked at the companions and they, too, were ready. She flicked her head in their direction as if to say, "Let's roll."

From a place of profound reverence and respect she approached her teachers. They embodied for her the razor thin line between the absurd, and the sublime. She knew now that the space in between hilarity and divinity was sacred. She felt grateful to the teachers for the gifts which they gave, and the woman also showed gratitude and gave praise to the One who first laughed and taught the magic of laughter to His world.

She went to her teachers, her masters, to seek their blessing and to consider thoughts of her journey ahead. But before she could give voice to the words of desire in her heart, one of the teaching masters walked purposely towards her, looked directly into the eyes of her soul, and sternly said, "You must leave now."

The woman was about to say something like, "Yes, I know, I was about to tell you the same thing and ask your blessing." But, before these words could come out, the master stopped even the thoughts in the woman's head. The master looked into the depth of her being and declared, "Your services here are no longer required."

The woman had forgotten how to fear, so fear was not an option, but there was confusion within her at this harsh change of tone coming from her teacher. The woman was about to ask the teacher a question when, once again, her teacher looked her straight in the eye and said, "You know who I am talking about, you know what needs to be done."

Suddenly, the woman became very aware; she knew then that the master was talking to and talking about a hurtful energy that still clung to life deep within her soul. The master was calling out the traveler's pride. Pride had been very far from the woman's mind, but apparently never completely removed from her being. All of the good she had experienced, all of the laughter, all of the beauty had been rendering pride's role in her life increasingly irrelevant.

The woman had softened so much, her true self strengthened so much, that pride had been inched away from its formerly commanding position. Weakened and ignored, pride was a mere shadow of its former self. Pride now teetered on the brink of complete expulsion, but it still existed. The teacher asked the woman to finish the job that had been started simply by her existing in this new world.

The woman looked within herself to see a twin shadow of being that she always had known lived within her but whose presence she had never wanted to acknowledge. Speaking from the power of the inner strength deep within her, she commanded her pride to come out of her and speak face to face. Given pride's weakened position, pride saw no reason to refuse. Her pride stepped out of her as naturally as someone steps out from behind a half-closed door.

At some level, the woman had known her whole life that pride covered her like a glove on a hand, but she never considered that it was a glove that she could, or would want to, take off. Pride had been so familiar to the woman that it had been literally hiding in plain sight this whole time.

In her old world, pride was thought to be something akin to narcissist self-promotion, grandiose attention grabbing and the putting on of supposed superior airs. What the women had come to realize was that pride had been a more subtle and dominant force. Pride was a quiet insistence that life follow its own expectations. Pride operated by persuading the woman to put herself at the center of the universe. Provide birthed and fostered a belief that the gifts of life were something that the woman had earned or achieved rather than gifts which she had received.

Pride told her, in its soft, seductive voice that even God could be at her beck and call, and that God should reward her good ideas and self-righteous intentions. Pride was clever; pride never denied God's existence, only His preeminence.

The woman could now see that Pride had relentlessly worked to flip her life script away from God. Pride made her believe that even prayer was a power of persuasion, a vehicle to convince God to empower the woman's agenda, and that her causes should always be advanced in her earth-life. Prayer was not a confession of dependency, but a subtle play at harnessing God's omnipotence for her own purposes.

The woman now knew how absurd this plan was. She also intuited that she was far from being alone, that many other humans sought to work with their pride to achieve a similar goal. Not surprisingly, God never bought into these plans, never gave pride what pride wanted. Sadly on earth, when a person was in lock step with pride's messaging, God was blamed for this "failure to care". God was given blame whenever He didn't deliver immediate gratification. Prayer had become a pitch for pride's will be done, pride's kingdom come. The woman had no idea how fully deceived she had been, how deeply pride choked out any true humility or faith.

Pride's propaganda had convinced the woman that she was pride's only benefactor in life, pride sold the notion that the woman was responsible to fight for pride's right to exist. Pride persuaded her that the woman's self-esteem would be compromised and greatly diminished if she abandoned it. Pride convinced her that if a little self-respect was good, then well-disguised superiority was even better. Pride offered itself as the woman's only true friend, that they alone knew right from wrong, that together they were the final arbiters of fairness and justice.

Eliminating the relevancy and role of God had been the greatest task of pride, and truth be told, pride had a remarkable *rate of success. With the woman's eyes now open to truth though, pride's days were numbered.*

With pride now fully revealed, the woman was uncertain how to finish the task of sending pride away forever. She moved to consult with her teachers about how best to proceed, what needed to be said and how she should say it. After looking deep within herself, and summoning up all of her humility and courage, the woman walked up to her pride, and started to talk to it as one would talk to a child or an old friend at the end of life.

She spoke slowly and purposely. She thanked her pride for its loyalty and devotion. She spoke of how important their relationship had been to her and they spoke of all the things that they had gone through together, all the secrets that they shared. She spoke to pride of how they knew each other in ways that no one else ever could, and that there was significance in that. She spoke to her pride about how important it had been to live life together and how glad she was that pride had always been there to share in it all with her. With a deep respect, the woman thanked pride for its service to her and the role that pride had sought to play as her protector.

Speaking as a mother might speak to her teenage daughter, she told to pride of how they both knew that someday this time would come, and that now was precisely the right time for this to be happening. Not making allowances for pride's ultimate harmful impact on her life, the woman took responsibility for her own foolishness and held out the truth that it was both she and pride together who had so grossly misread the purpose of life.

Speaking firmly now like a teacher to a pupil, or a coach to a player, the woman commanded that pride leave. Pride could leave with its head held high, with the dignity and honor that it deserved. Pride did not move, so speaking from the fire in her eyes, the woman simply said, "Leave now."

Pride jumped out of immediate view like a shadow vanishing in light. Still sensing pride's lingering presence, the

A LIFE in the DAY of HEAVEN

woman spoke out an important truth revealed to her by her teachers. She told pride that, now without human form, it would be easier for it to make its own journey into the eternal realm, and to find its own path to redemption. Pride was to be free of her, as much as she was to be free of it. Pride didn't need her, and she didn't need it, she never did. Pride could now travel into the place of beauty and silence and find relief and joy unimaginable. Pride could find the kind of peace which the woman had found.

There has been no further response from her pride, and pride's presence still invisibly hovered in her midst. With the final outcome still hanging in the balance, the low rumble of a growl came from one of the lions. Pride then left quickly, gone on its way to find its own destiny and completion, gone with no way of ever returning to haunt and seduce.

Another in a series of indescribably deep, cleansing breaths came out of the core of woman's being. She had woken up in this world, in her dwelling place with a sense of pure liberation and freedom, and yet each new part of the journey, each new experience, had left her feeling evermore free, evermore complete. It was like looking at a canvas of disarming purity, a dazzling display of white, only for a canvas emerging from beyond the starting point that somehow was even whiter, and purer, and cleaner. This happened over and over again to her. She possessed an ever-expanding capacity to feel delight and satisfaction.

Redirecting her attention to the scene around her, she realized that she was still at the edge of the lake, she was still with her teachers, and she was still with her companions. She stood and basked in the sheer pleasure of the beauty around her and the wonder of the continuous birthing of her true self. She felt, again, the energy to move, but unlike before, it emerged as relaxed and patient, with no hint of a rush.

The woman felt so solid, so integrated, and so light all at the same time. Every part of her continued to love every other part of herself without competition or conflict. She smiled at her *companions, she said goodbye to her teachers, and they were on their way, off to journey even deeper into eternal beauty.*

This is where the dreams stopped. This was the last dream of heaven that I was to dream.

A LIFE in the DAY of HEAVEN

CHAPTER TEN

I continue to rummage through the notes and tapes and memories of that time, remnants of thoughts born through those sessions with Meg. I had forgotten the hope and wonder that the dreams inspired. The dreams were and are incredibly impactful. I am so pleased that the reading of these dreams still seems to recalibrate something profound in me, just as they did so long ago. I regret losing touch with them; I remain surprised that I had just walked away from them without continuing to celebrate their value.

Many things about this time of my life surprise me, even to this day. As I remember the whole of what was going on with the dreams, with my time with Meg, with my sermons, I am shocked to recall just how alternately beautiful and unseemly the whole story had been. For example, how could I, at the time of the most profoundly spiritual weeks of my life, how could I be so foolish, immature and dark? I was truly blind, and I am perplexed by the contrasting emotions which rage in and around us as human beings. My contradictions, my duplicity, seem to have no end, at least not on this side of eternity.

A LIFE *in the* DAY *of* HEAVEN

What I should have done, what I still need to do, is pay more attention to the dream story. In the dream story of the woman in Heaven, I saw pride revealed not just as a passing fancy, but a physical life force which had woven its way into every pore of the woman's being. She was, and is, a good person and yet pride played on her fears so relentlessly that the voice of woman's life song had been seriously usurped by pride's siren song.

I suspect that my true life song had been similarly hijacked. Why would I be any different? The preeminence of pride in human life as a parallel life force would certainly explain some of my duplicity. For example, I see pride in my attitudes about achieving professional success. I mock myself for my lack of success, but the self-mocking is more of a way to diffuse fear and pain, there is more going on than meets the eye. The importance of success in my life, in my eyes, can't be overstated. I guess so much depends on how success is defined.

Professionally speaking, I have defined success as being a person of impact. The imagined joy in having both great (affecting many people) and good (positive) impact has been the dream vision of my life, but I can see that my quest for success has run afoul of an impure heart. There are no excuses for somethings, but there are reasons for most. If I allow for the strong probability that pride infects every good human intention, I can see why even my dream of great and good success has been compromised.

The compromise comes via an additional ingredient which I, somewhere in time forgotten, added to my goal of having great and good impact in the lives of others. The ingredient added to my dream of success is that my success is only truly realized when I get the credit for it. I'm the one who must get the attention; I'm the one who must be seen as orchestrator and implementer of good. My cunning is so complete that I will gladly give God some credit, but only after I am seen front and center. It is on those terms will I share the stage. How insidious is this evil in me? These attitudes are a violation of sacred truths, and I cringe as I see this confession put to words. It's small solace as I instinctively reassure myself that vain foolishness is not unique to me

I'm aware of this vanity in me because I've learned to pay attention to the shifting shadows of thoughts inside my head. Paying focused attention to subtle shifts in motivation is the only way that I've come to see the pride in me. The voice of God is still and small, but the influence of pride is a whispered suggestion, a camouflaged but deadly nudge. It has taken me years now to recognize the thread of pride's voice and to, in my own way, call pride out. My outing of in me comes through journaling. Putting to pen the seduction of pride's whispers is my own form of protest and resistance to the pride's deceptions.

As I have journaled out my feelings over the years, I see a strange phenomenon as I wrestle with the beauty and danger of professional acclaim. In writing out my threads of thoughts, I can see this odd ability to simultaneously elevate and diminish God in my heart and mind. God, please forgive me. I can see a mixture of sincere faith and profound distrust running side by side, both racing to cross the finish line before the other.

For example, I have complete confidence in God's goodness and protection. I believe that God would grant me the satisfaction of being a difference maker in my community if my peculiar definition of success was not so detrimental to my soul. He protects me from myself. If I would only just celebrate the meaning in being used and drop the poison of selfish expectations, then I am certain that success would find its way to my doorstep. God is a giver of good gifts; He is the true conduit to good change. The insistence that my ego be fed through the process is not.

My selective, yet profound faith in God drives the emotional angst of my inner conflict. I believe God to be the only vehicle which drives the right blend of impact and good in life. His power is the fuel that runs the vehicle of beauty, but the price of such power must seem high in my distorted way of thinking because His glory is not my first thought, and I'm not sure if it's even a distance second. The theological rub here is that God is not shy about declaring that all of life exists to and for His glory, so in a weird way my faith reinforces my fear is that He will be glorified and not me. The thought that glory is His alone pokes a stick in the sleeping animal. His glory alone threatens to drain the power of an ungodly hibernating beast still a deeply imbedded in secret caves. The survival instinct in me still fights to justify my existence by gaining more points on some gigantic cosmic scorecard. More points than even God. I feel guilty that I do not trust Him more.

Why does His glory, His good and perfect will, frighten me? Am I afraid of being relegated to hallways of anonymity like portraits on a castle wall? Would He grind my need for self-importance on the mortar of His holiness into invisibility? Under my pride's spell, I act as if my success is the proverbial tree that falls unseen in the philosophical forest, I act as if I don't get full credit then success should never happen at all. But why do I feel this way? Success does not have to be binary, how did I get to such a place of an all or nothing tussle with God?

Further heightening the absurdity of all of these worries is the fact that I have no real understanding of what it would be like to be even marginally famous anyway. How do I know what I would feel should my dreams, however compromised they may be, come true? I might find that I am more capable of feeling humility and gratitude than I realize. Also, while I crave the fantasized adulation that would come with success, I don't know what it would really be like. I don't know if pressures to perform or constraints on the freedom of privacy, etc. outweigh the pleasure. I don't know, but I've always wanted to find out.

It's weird to see these attitudes in me. I have no doubt in God's goodness and power, but I guess I don't really trust in His right to define what is good for me. Quite a presumptuous thought don't you think? It seems as though a part of me believes my definition of good to be superior to His. A part of me is also shockingly certain that He would deny me any real joy in His success. These attitudes are actually the antithesis of what I believe.

My core faith in the artful partnering between God and people was shaped by the most powerful of sermons. Years ago I was on a strange journey and I found myself in a steaming, colorfully decorated, open sky Church in the island country of Sri Lanka. The pastor there poured out his thundering truth over and over again "When God is most gloried, then I am most satisfied." His voice and his heart rose up and down perfectly in sync with the flow of his words, "When God is most glorified, then I am most satisfied." The pastor would wander in and out of contemplative thought, only to return again to rock solid conviction of "When God is most glorified, then I am most satisfied." What he preached that day is what I believe, I still can hear the pastor's words, but I see a different attitude in my heart. I carry a fear of God; a distrust of His will, how ridiculous is that? I'm afraid of the sustainability of His mercy, oh ya, He's been right so far, but what about the next time. I'm afraid that He doesn't know me as well as I know myself. I forget that He made me.

Maybe I should have listened to what I preached. Maybe this mistrust of God is example of the reality of the God-trauma theory that I spoke of from my pulpit. Maybe I'm afraid that the shadow cast by His good work accomplished leaves me invisible, maybe I'm afraid of being cast to the gutter as His parade marches down the center of the street to the applause of thousands. Maybe I feel some tremor of the rippling disaster of Adam and Eve's expulsion, and like them I fear ending up on the wrong side of the gates of Eden.

I don't know. I just know that pride and fear conspire together to form a lethal front against wisdom and beauty in this world. Sometimes I think that if only I could live long enough, I could figure out the formula needed to fully extricate myself from the foundations of my folly. I wish that, like the woman in the Heaven dreams, I could cast out these demons of destruction. Upon reflection however, who do I think that I am? I conveniently forget that the Heaven woman had a lot of help, so even my thought that I could defeat my pride is in and of itself an example of pride's strength in me.

I guess we don't get to live life here with the foresight of future knowledge. I guess we don't know what we don't know, until we know it. It's just that some of the words which I've written scare me. I'm afraid that history will not look kindly on me (again, a wild distortion of my own importance) I just wish I could edit out some of the embarrassment of my foolishness, but, I will not take that liberty. With the image of life's tapestries in mind, I'm banking on the belief that even my flaws added some flavor, however dark and sour, to the recipe of this story. Maybe failure truly is the greatest success in life.

Enough with all of this introspection, I have work still to do. There will be time to sift through all of my questions and conflicts; I need now to get back to the task at hand. I want to get the rest of this story out. I've played almost all of the session tapes in the box and I'm still looking for some healing resolution to come by virtue of this labor.

Looking back on my notes, I remember that when Meg came in for her next session, she was in a bad way. She had a hard time sitting still, her eyes darted around the room; she was breathing heavy and fast. It was like this for most of the times that we met, she would often begin in an agitated state. Usually however, she would wait for me to begin, but this time she launched right into telling her story. "Something has changed," she said. "It reminds me of that old book, 'It was the best of times, and it was the worst of times.'"

"Oh, that's Dickens," I offered, trying to offer up my own interpretation of nonchalance. Instead of dealing with the nightmare of our last session, I was bandaging up open wounds without treatment, hoping that ignoring the poison would weaken it.

"Great, okay, A-plus schoolboy… now can you shut-up and just try to listen?" she retorted.

I could never seem to do enough things right in her eyes, yet she always seemed so needy of me, so expectant of something wonderful to be given to her by me. It was confusing.

"I feel like…" Her eyes softened. "I feel like my insides are being reworked, they are all tangled up. I'm being pushed forward, I can't draw back, I can't bury my feelings, I can't hide my fears."

"I'm sorry." I immediately regret interrupting her. "You seemed to be doing so much better." I had defaulted to my familiar posture of meaningless babble, a weak stab at empathy gone awry. Whether real or auto-pilot, apologizing was to Meg was the itch that I was compelled to scratch. I always felt that I was to blame for anything negative she felt. If I had a masochistic need to be blamed, Meg was always happy to oblige me, and play the part of the critic.

"Why don't you get it?" she screamed. "How is it that you, supposedly an expert on the soul, why do you know so little about it?"

Her accusations mirror the echoes of my own self-loathing and I all but hung my head in shame.

She started to talk slowly, as one spoke to a child, but this time her manner was without cruelty. She said, "Please hear me, I'm changing, my old ways of hiding myself are not working anymore. This is hard, but it's good." She paused, she seemed to want to stop, but she pushed forward. "Suffering is required here on this earth, maybe not in heaven, but here—suffering is real. It is necessary, don't you understand that?"

Then her voice rose again in real anger as she sensed a softening between us. "You're a Christian, for Christ's sake; do you know Him, really know Him? Do you know His life? Men came to murder Him the night He was born. They came to slaughter Him at His first breath. None of this "Little Town of Bethlehem" bull. Do you not know His suffering? Do you not know that He said that you must die in order to live, to really live?" She appraised me—she looked me up and down, as if examining a piece of fruit at the grocery store. "You're a child." This was the verdict of her assessment.

Eventually she moved on from her critique of me, as if bored by it all, and gave me more of her story.

"My dad raised me after my mom left us. He was a good man; he had a way about him, never running too hot or too cold. He was my sweet daddy, the safest of men. After he died, being put into the foster care system, well, you can imagine how much I hated it. My dad had loved me, believed in me, gave me all of himself. Now, I was either getting bounced away from one dysfunctional family to another… or stuck in a group home with other kids that nobody wanted. I can see now that I made it difficult for anyone to want me, but I didn't know that then. I was just always mad.

"People in the system, foster families, and social workers etc. were always referring to us foster kids as 'kiddos' or 'buckaroos' like we were some cute little bundles of sunshine. Well, I, for one, was not. It might come as a surprise to you, but I was not always easy to be around."

She then smiled just enough to show me that she was self-aware enough to know that she was still not easy to be with.

She continued with her story, "Labeling children as 'kiddos' always felt like someone was trying to make us more pleasant sounding, more digestible to regular people. Being called a 'kiddo' really just felt that someone was putting a target on my back, announcing to the world that I was not normal, at least that how I felt."

She paused, caught her breath, and said, "I don't think that I have told you this, but I work with kids who have been traumatized by their foster care experiences. I sit down and hold their pain, suffer their rage. They are not 'kiddos,' they are not cute little orphan children like in 'Oliver Twist'."

I wanted to say, "Ah, another Dickens novel, I'm sensing a theme." I wanted to be corny and cute, another default defense of mine. Usually I was addicted to any chance of making a stab at the challenge of walking the line between stupid and clever. Instead I just shut up and stayed quiet. Maybe I was learning.

Meg went on. "People have the wrong idea about kids, they tend to ignore them or idealize them. I love the kids that I work with, but I get so mad at them too, they can be such brats, so I call them on their crap. The thing that is best about them is that they keep things real. You know where you stand with them, and they want to know where they stand with you.

"The best that I can offer them is to be real back. These kids have seen too much, they've had to grow up way too fast. They bounce back and forth between acting older than their age or regressing to some kind of infantile state. When they really suffer though is when they can't assess the emotional climate of what they see around them. Misinterpreting the intentions of the caregivers, who is safe, who is not safe, any miscalculations can trigger devastating consequences. The kids are so hungry for love, but they are so afraid that their appetite is too great, that their hunger will be too repulsive for others to tolerate.

"I bet you are good at what you do," I had offered up, perhaps for the first time, a compliment that I really meant. It was not some gratuitous fluff that was said just to be likeable.

"I get real results," she answered. "I'm good, but it's really hard. There is just so much hurt, it keeps coming day and day. I feel their suffering, I see their anger, and I take a certain amount of emotional abuse from them. They give it to me because I'm safe, I won't lash out or retaliate, and they need to know that."

I reply, "You get emotionally beat up, unfairly treated because you are emotional safe; yeah I know how that feels." Sarcasm was not a wise choice, especially in light of what we were talking about. I immediately regretted what I said.

She lashed out at me, "Oh, my God, can you not make everything about you? Just one time, get over yourself. Look, I know I have high expectations, I'm sure I expect a lot because I give so much of myself to the kids, but my gosh, buck up, stop whining, stop feeling sorry for yourself. I see some honesty in you and you deserve honesty from me. So, just let me talk, okay? Don't compete, don't apologize, just listen."

I felt like a fool, but I'm not fighting this, so I just simply said, "Okay."

"If you would have paid attention more to your own spiritual pulse," she said. "If you had more real understanding of spiritual processes, you would know some things. You would know that spiritual gains do not get built like a brick wall gets built. It is not one layer achieved which is then solid enough for the next understanding to be added on top of it. It's not that concrete.

The spiritual process is not like a great river, always pushing forward; it is more like the tides of the ocean, surging forward and then retreating, back and forth, highs and lows." She stopped, and sighed.

It was clear that she was in some conflict. Being anxious in the silence and tension of unresolved emotion I blurted out, "Perhaps we can just go back to how it was when we last met."

Turning dark before me, she snarled, "Which part? The part where I felt clear, and whole, and lovely, or the part where you dared me to show you just how weak your precious façade really is?

"I don't get you. I have this clarity, I'm sitting here last week in a good place for a change, and you beg for the shadow in me to come out, you seductive little sniffling peon. I then tell you that the game that you want to play is too much for you, and that any kind of nonsense will cost both of us a lot. I'm doing all of the work, again. I spell it out for you, remember, but you don't care. You just had to prove something to me, or to yourself, or whatever, and we both get pulled down your toilet."

I deserved every last drop of her rage. I can see her working not to destroy me and I'm shamed by her efforts.

"You were so out of line. I'm just trying to get over it. I was in a good place before last time, yes that's true. My spirit was full, and my shadows were silent. This happens sometimes, but the good place is fleeting. I just want to stay with some sort of peace, and yes I expect you to help me get there, not rip it away from me." She sadly shook her head and that was the unkindest cut of all. "For me, it's like God's Spirit fills me, in this case, your dreams bless me, heal me, but then because the cup in my heart is filled with tiny holes, the peace drips out and I run dry. I can't trust you. Not only are you not safe like my sweet father was, you don't even see how truly dangerous you are."

Of course, I understand some of what she is saying, but some of it I don't. I know that she has a more eloquent spiritual vocabulary; she is verbally more expressive of her emotions, probably from spending all that time talking to foster kids, but some of what she said seemed like nonsense. Still wanting to be useful, the only words that I came up with turned out to be not useful at all. "Tell me what to say, tell me what to do."

Her voice rose again. "I'm tired of being in charge. I'm tired of being the child whisperer for abused kids, and I sure don't want to be some kind of spiritual muse for my pastor. I want somebody to be a grown-up for me, to do for me what I do for these kids. I want someone to whisper back to me, to whisper something useful and wise. You have authority, you lust for followers, you want attention. Well, if you want followers, then lead, damn it. You want me to follow? Please lead."

I desperately tried to think of what I should say. I tried to think about what other pastors would say. Instead, out of nowhere wisdom showed up. I started talking about the dreams. Instead of trying to create something out of thin air, or try to prove myself again, I decided to use what had been given to me to use. I had prayed to Him for guidance, for miracles, one has been given, and suddenly, it makes sense to just keep it simple and use the gift given.

I never should have played amateur shrink. I should have just stayed with the dreams—they had given her much needed comfort and wisdom. Apart from the dreams, comfort and wisdom were not tools that I had in my toolbox. I could reach for them all day long and still come up empty.

I didn't possess the right kind of love and maturity then, especially when confronted with such a complicated woman like Meg. What became suddenly clear was that I couldn't give what wasn't mine to give her. I had nothing, and in that moment, I reluctantly gave up my battle with her. Seeing the existential truth of my own emotional lack somehow inspired me to finally find the right note on the emotional keyboard.

I confessed to her that I thought that she was right, that these dreams had just as much to do with her as they had to do with me. I said that they were given to both of us. I also told her that I've not shared the dream with anybody partially because I was afraid to, but also because I knew all along that the dreams were for her. My part in her story was that I was meant to give her the dreams as a gift.

I asked her which part of the dream story has resonated most within her. I asked her what part of the dreams most reminded her of herself. She told me what connected most deeply with her. I mentioned what had resonated most deeply in me. We compared thoughts and insights. We talked about the dreams back and forth for a long time.

I confessed to Meg that there was a reason that I had held back agreeing with her about the dreams being meant for both of us, not just me. I told Meg that I felt such a strong attachment to the dream traveler and I was afraid to diminish in any way my special relationship with her. I wanted the dream traveler all to myself; I didn't want to share her. I told Meg that she had been right to call out my possessiveness and we laughed at the absurdity that I even wanted to emotionally own the dearly departed. Meg was just quirky enough to get a kick out of my confession and she relaxed in the face of my transparency.

We wondered together about whether other people would find meaning in the dreams. I told her that I had considered that also. I also shared that in light of our new understanding that we both shared a spiritual copyright position, that I wouldn't share the Heaven dreams without her permission. She thanked me for that thoughtfulness, and offered the opinion that I should share them with my congregation at some point. We both said *goodbye* after an hour of peacefully talking together, both feeling refreshed and satisfied.

I closed the door, needing space and quiet to put my thoughts in order. I felt that there was something to learn in all that had just happened with Meg and me. I should have realized all along that it was the path of humility which led to good results. Whenever I stopped fighting, whenever I stopped competing, that is when a good, healthy connection took place. There were times when I heard the whispers of vulnerability telling me to slow down, to be still and let some things be unknown, but I was a slave to my habits. I was a habitual overachiever and I thought that my role as a pastor to her was to model certainty, not vulnerability.

Comfortably ensconced in my head, I had retreated from the rawness of feeling. I had been unwilling to accept that I was not capable of being in control of every situation and circumstance. I was trying to learn new lessons, but finding that, like Meg, I too had little holes in my wisdom bucket.

Looking back, I find it ironic that I prayed to God that He would give me the kind of emotional presence and stamina that Meg had, and yet, each time I had the chance just to sit with the brutal edge of real emotion and live in faith, I retreated. Every time I prayed for spiritual muscles, God gave me emotional barbells to bench press and then I walked away from them, intimidated by their heft, leaving them untouched and leaving myself alone to complain of my feebleness.

I imagined that I didn't linger long in that time of emotional introspection. I'm sure that I shortly withdrew to focus my energies to write my next sermon. I remembered that there had been a bit of buzz about those sermons. The academics in the crowd were intrigued. There had been a couple of theological thresholds breached, in their opinion, and they were debating the merits of potential new spiritual ground. But, at this point, I seemed to be running out of new material, it's kind of like I had the equivalent of a creative thunderstorm and

A LIFE in the DAY of HEAVEN

now the outpouring was just a sprinkle of intellectual showers. The bottom line is that I had forty minutes of content to fill and I was more than a little short.

A little voice spoke to my heart and said, "Share the dreams." That voice really shook me. I know that Meg and I had talked about sharing our dreams to the congregation, but that seemed hypothetical, this felt real.

I was still not completely able to see the dreams as a gift; a part of me wanted credit for generating something powerful on my own accord. I still wanted to be the focus, not them, but some other part of me also didn't want to be known as the whacko who dreamed dreams. I wanted to be respectable. I wanted the awe that came with a title like "creative genius", but I remained risk avoidant. As it related to sharing the dreams with the congregation, the term "professional suicide" also crossed my mind.

These are the notes I spoke from of this, the last of the sermon notes, which I had buried in the box.

#1 OUR BROKENNESS

Life here is hard. The consequences of the Fall of Adam are curses, death, pain, and pride. There is not much beauty here now, especially when compared to the incalculable eon of Paradise, which still stands as foundational to our human experience. Dark are the days, darker still are our sleeping souls, muted is our dignity, spiritual hibernation has become our norm.

But despite all traumas, and the blindness which has followed, dark is neither the essence of our being, nor of the essence of our destiny. Eternal light and love lie ahead, with the hiccup of dark only now temporarily dominant.

God is beauty, and all things He has created have beauty at its essence. Beauty is what He makes; beauty is what He restores all things to—no present darkness will be able to resist this. Beauty is the starting pointing, beauty is the finish line and beauty is our path in between. We might as well get best acquainted with His ways and the dominant ways of divine Beauty, because they will quickly become the whole of our life experience. The ways of faith, hope and love will soon become our eternal currency, the one and only coinage of the realm.

Darkness will not even be a memory for us to linger over. Darkness will become as foreign as true majesty, love and light is to us now. For now however, we have much inside of us that needs healing. There is much inside of us that needs to relax, take a breath and smile. There is a great need for that which is soulful, eternal, and spiritual in us to recalibrate back to our Creator and Sustainer. We need alignment with life, ourselves, and others in new ways, ways which reflect the truths which we hold so dear, yet forget so quickly.

#2 HEALING

I believe that a mind set on Heaven offers a hope of bringing the kind of soul altering spiritual recalibrations that we need to experience His light in this dark place. It is not my intention to shock you, believe me I don't, but I need to say that what I speak of today, I speak from my own experience. Some experiences are ones which I will share with you later.

I believe that our life healing greatly accelerates through what the Bible calls "storing your treasures in Heaven" and by "setting your sights on the things above". Storing treasures in Heaven involves a willingness to invest energy in the pursuit of the Heavenly realm, to invest in its beauty, in its values. Setting your sights on the things above involves an intentional envisioning of Heaven, an active practice of imaging now our forever life to come. A spiritual mentor of mine once trained me in the art of living each day with eternity's values clearly in focus. I had forgotten that practice until just recently.

Don't be afraid of your imagination; just school it for your benefit. Imagination is not fantasy. Imagination can be just as real and just as gloriously beneficial as anything else as long as it is properly applied. Imagination, like all things, exists to and for the glory of God, but like all things it can be misapplied. The proper purpose of imagination is to increase our wonder of Him and hunger for Him.

The misapplication of imagination is that, in the service of pride, imagination might not fuel the wonder of His power, but a wish for our own. The Bible speaks of "vain imaginations" which are defined as ways of seeking our own glory. Vain are our imaginations when we fantasize of our own power, when we create pictures in our heads of life and the circumstances which we desire to seize ourselves, rather than wait on God to give that which is truly essential. Too often, these are fantasized wishes designed to place us solidly on the center seat of self-importance. We insist that God conform to the realities of the life scripts which we have written in our hearts. We spin tales of glory in our own minds as if our wishes can act as the power of God and create realities of our own making.

Power driven vain imaginations are today's equivalence of the ancient, tragic thought that "we can be like the Most High". A humble Imagination of Heaven, a humble imagination of wonder, is the celebration of the simple reality that we can't ever be God, and that we exist for His story, for His glory Can you see the differences here on how imagination can be used and miss-used? These differences are subtle but they are significant.

The bible teaches that "Whatever is true, whatever is noble, whatever is right, whatever is pure, whatever is lovely, whatever is admirable—if anything is excellent or praiseworthy—think about such things." I want to paint some lovely, pure, praiseworthy images to imagine, some possibilities to consider. The images of Heaven can humble and soothe, excite and delight. The images of heaven are shared with the hope and prayer of, Jesus invited us to call down the beauty of Heaven, "Thy Kingdom come, Thy will be done on earth as it is in heaven."

Let the prayer "Heaven now" tune your hearts to the better things beyond.

We can't change what happened in the past, many things cannot be undone, but we can alter our responses and minimize the toxicity. Misapplied imaginations of power wish to shape circumstances in alignment with omnipotent wishes. Humble imaginations of God's wonder drive to take the sting out of death and the cursed circumstances of earth-life.

Your imagination is an instrument of transportation. Your imagination will take you either to places of riches or ruin, it's up to you. Please know that your imagination meter is always running, always taking you somewhere, so pay close attention and make an intentional choice.

One of the purposes of utilizing the imagination in the treatment of trauma is this element of choice, this power of intention. We don't have to be victims of our human lineage; we can break free of some of the chains. We can detach ourselves from bondage to the ways of the world as the arbitrators of success, and see that Heavenly success is defined not by earth-life circumstances, but by God-developed character of joy.

Character is the summation of our life experience, not something that we strain to create, but something that we partner with God to receive. Character, Godly character, is less about morality, less about willpower and more about the impact and quality of our experiences of our soul altering, spirit healing with Him. Godly character, the experience of Him is what sets us to soar.

With the quality of God experiences in mind, I want to shift our attention now to an experience that I've had of Him, an experience that I've had of and with His Kingdom. An experience of His Heaven which is now, and the same Heaven which is ours to come.

We are instructed to "Set our sights on the things above, not on the things that are of earth." Right now, let the setting of your sights on the things above not be an intellectual consideration, but an emotional hunger. Travel with me, and consider the things above. In the spirit of this verse and others, and with the full understanding that what I will share is in the realm of mystery, I want to tell you a story. This is a true story of how Heaven has visited me. What I will tell you is neither an authoritative summation of Heaven, nor a claim of revelation. Rather, this is a story of my own actual experience of what I perceive to be the Heavenly realm.

#3 DREAMS????

These are where my notes end, but I know that my sermon did not end here. This was the day when I told the congregation of my dreams. You can tell by my last sermon heading (Dreams????) that I remained ambivalent about even sharing my story up to the very end, but shared it I did. I shared with them snippets of what I had seen, heard and felt from the dream traveler's journey. I felt the air being pressed out of the room the moment I began to talk. I felt none of the beauty that I was describing, I only felt that I was making an obvious mistake, visible to everyone else, but not to me.

I had assumed that I had already taken the more provocative risk in talking about "God Trauma." I thought if raising the possibility that somehow God could be a source of trauma (even though I hope by now you know that the phrase "God Trauma" has nothing whatsoever with finding fault with God) didn't incite the villagers to riot, then nothing would. I was wrong.

My congregation was always up for theology, for a little intellectual thrust and parry, but they were not prepared for the emotionality of their pastor receiving dreams of heaven from God. It was not, per se, that they found fault with the nature of, or the images from, heaven. What got the congregation all wound was the alleged crossover of the supernatural realm into my life, and by extension into their lives as well. If they accepted the dreams from me as being from God, then what would be next? Would there be people dancing in the spirit and speaking in strange tongues? Would there be pandemonium in the pews? Would syrupier voiced southern preachers now want to make our Church part of their carnival circuit rounds? Things could, in the minds of some, get out of hand real quick.

So, the message of heaven was right, but the messenger's means of communication, God talking to me, was wrong. He wasn't supposed to act in such a familiar way with me, and if He did, I certainly was not supposed to talk about it. Look but don't touch, see but don't say, this apparently was part of the unwritten which polite evangelical pastors never saw, but were judged by nevertheless. It was all a bunch of sanctimonious nonsense.

Ultimately, I don't really know if my decision to be transparent about my dreams came from conviction or courage, or if I just needed filler for the rest of my sermon. I know that I had consulted with Meg about telling my story of theses dreams, but I really didn't decide until I was in the moment. Was it the right decision? Like in many things, I don't know. I didn't know then, and I don't know now.

I also didn't know how to fully understand my heaven dreams theologically. There were things that I saw and heard which didn't fit quite neatly into the tight box of my preconceptions. So, again, I don't know. One thing that I've learned from the Scripture is that everyone who assumed that they fully knew the workings of God and the meaning of His Word were proved to be shortsighted. All through-out the God story, I could see the historical folly of deciding for God exactly how He is to work in the world. Many biblical characters were shocked to see that God was not constrained by their preconception of how He should exist in this, His creation.

On the other hand, there seemed to be special grace in the Bible for those whom admitted their ignorance and weakness. Grace of any kind was running in short supply in my life so I chose to confess that I didn't have all of the answers. "I don't know" became my honest answer when pressed to defend my story and my thoughts.

I believe that admitting that you "don't know" is one, truthful, and two a decidedly Christian thing to say (faith, "the assurance of things not seen, of things not known", that kind of thing). Be that as it may, my fear was that for a pastor to say that they don't have ready answers for any and all spiritual questions doesn't earn one philosophical style points. A lack of theological decisiveness often equates to a short shelf life in the ministry. These were thoughts for me to ponder.

In any case, there was uproar from the community within and around our Church. I had taken spontaneity and inspiration out for a spin without parental permission and I got my hand slapped for it. While my congregation was accepting of my use of the descriptor of "God-Trauma", greater Christendom was not. There were stories given to the press by biblical scholars that I had "Opened Pandora's Box", that I was "leading the charge of representing humans as victims of God's cruelty." This could not be further from the truth. How absurd. I was even tempted to go on the attack and lash out, to defend God's good name, but truth be told, I was probably more concerned about defending mine own.

I felt accosted by two battle fronts, my congregation's distress over my foray into the supernatural and academic Christendom's assault on my Biblical scholarship, or lack thereof. Any military leader will tell you that fighting a two front war is a losing proposition and I succumbed to the siren call of retreat. In the fog of theological battle I froze, I didn't know what to do, so I did nothing.

A wise person in my life came to me, and I'll never forget him showing up at my back door in the midst of all of this nonsense. He said, "There is a price that will be paid here." He said that when Bob Dylan sang, "I would not feel so all alone, everybody must get stoned," that he was not necessarily just singing about weed, he was even more singing of the dangerous path of a prophet, whether that prophet be social, political, or religious. My friend said that anyone willing to stand outside of the camp of the conventional was going to be a target, so I could either give up the soapbox or lose my job.

I asked him, "What's the price of not speaking of such things as dreams and Heaven?"

He said that I would lose the voice, that the Spirit would find another person to speak through, to dream through.

It was a no-brainer for me; I would move on from the supernatural, I would keep my job. For the next five weeks, I taught a series I entitled, "The Wisdom of Proverbs; Practical Applications for the Twenty-First Century Christian." And the controversy died. I killed it with conventionality.

I remember that there was about a month's time when I heard nothing at all from Meg. I had heard nothing further from God either, the well had run dry. One day, as I sat contemplating my next sermon, trying to get everything in order, I received a package from Meg. She had sent to me a copy of her personal diary entries. She showed me a massive amount of trust in doing this, and I was touched.

I read her thoughts, dreams, and feelings. This was all Meg, there was nothing censored or contrived. She was far from flattering to me in what she wrote, but it was all much more digestible to me from a distance rather than close up and personal. There was also little of the anger and rancor of the past. Most of her entries were sweet and wise, full of insight and beauty. She had sustained her health. The seeds of peace had taken root and were growing.

She said that she had been hesitant to show me evidence of healing, she was afraid that showing me her growth would jinx it all. In typical Meg fashion, she pushed through her fear, and I was blessed to hear of her joy.

She requested one more face to face time, a time to say goodbye. My last session with Meg was actually very sweet. I was certain then that the slaying of the shadows in Meg would be a lasting condition. There could be no denying that a corner had been turned.

Meg had the whole set of dreams on tape to listen to at her discretion. Those tapes had become the north point on the emotional compass of her life. When she felt herself falter in any way, she could recalibrate herself to the timelessness of eternity and the joy therein. She had written to me that whenever she was afraid or feeling on edge, she would listen to the tapes of the dreams; imagine her Heavenly companions around her, slow down her breathing and step forward on her journey in humility and gratitude. What a lovely way to live, how strange that she found the pathway to her peace through such a flawed vessel such as myself.

Meg and I had had shared some rough and tough times together, I was so ashamed of my bad behavior during our one especially dark session. I remember being in the throes of confusion and remorse for days. One night I stole into the dark corner of my home office and wrote to her a desperate letter. I told her that I was a failure, that I could not give her what she deserved. I meant every word of it. She wrote back, saying that that it was not what I did or didn't have to give, it was never me that held any hopeful promise to her, it was us. There was something in our connection that she couldn't explain. If Meg couldn't find words for why ultimately we were good for each other, I certainly couldn't even begin to guess. I guess it was sort of the whole being greater than the sum of the parts kind of thing.

She did say that this is the way which God works, His redemption is never given in a vacuum, and relationships are always the vehicles of transformation. It was our chemistry which created just the right kind of recipe for healing. She told me that she was the spark which triggered the Heaven in me, and I was the dreamer who shaped the roar of her fire into a sustainable glow.

I remember one time that she compared our relationship to the story of the prophet Balaam in the Old Testament. In that story, Balaam is a prophet who had lost his way, who had decided not to live out his calling. He was lost and floundering.

Correction and direction came to the prophet through an unexpected source. It was a good talking to from the mouth of Balaam's donkey which got the prophet back on the right path. In the best of who Meg was, as she told me that story of the wayward prophet, she added with a twinkle in her eye, "I let you decide which of us is the prophet and which of is the ass."

I guess I was a bit of both prophet and ass. I was humbled that something of great value had come to her through me. It was my voice that was painting those pictures of beauty and hope, it was my eyes seeing Eternity on full display and then finding the words to express the inexpressible. I was there; I saw the miracle of truly being born-again. Perhaps the truest miracle however, was how the sublime maneuvered through all of my emotional flaws. How beautiful was it to behold that good was able to survive the mixture of profound and profane that marked those days of Meg and I together.

Strangely, it turned out that Meg and I were practically the only ones to benefit from these dreams. Under the pen name of Louis Warren, I had written a pretty complete version of this story down to gage public interest. I even got a Christian publishing house to put it out in print. The response was decidedly underwhelming. There were, literally, dozens of people who claimed varying degrees of deliverance from meditating on the dreams, and hearing the story. Yes, you read right, dozens, not hundreds, dozens, not thousands, dozens, not millions… dozens. Oh well, mass commercial appeal remains elusive. Timing is always everything and looking back, I am satisfied with the majority of outcomes which came my way in my life.

Meg spoke of her father in our last session. She said that I was like her father, in that I dreamed of big things, but could just never find the right canvas on which to best express the inspiration. Her father was a want-to-be singer/songwriter who could never get on the right side of anything remotely resembling a hit. Meg told me that she had been thinking about us and thinking about some of her father's old country western songs.

She said that there was one song of his which was running like a looped recording in her head.

She told me the lyric, but one verse really stood out. The verse went like this, "A wino needs his bottle, a hero needs his fall, and if the two get all mixed up, well you can chuck it all. They both need something special, a kiss upon the cheek, to keep them bouncing off the gutter, and headed for the street."

She said that this is how she saw her life now; she was bouncing off the gutter and headed for the street.

True to myself to the end I said, "Heading for the street sounds dangerous to me."

Meg said, "Well, the gutter's not such a great option either. At least the street is a place which gets you from here to there, otherwise we just stay stuck." She thought for a moment more and said, "Thank you, pastor. Everyone, dark and light, wise and foolish, needs the kiss upon the cheek, you gave that to me. I would like to think that I kissed your cheek as well. A kiss of something divine, that is rare in this world." With that said, she lightly kissed me on the check and left. That was the last that I would ever hear from her or about her.

I sat here thinking, who was Meg to me? Was she the woman in the gospel story caught in lies, the woman of scandal whom Jesus stood with at the water well, or was she the angel who stirred the healing waters at the pool of Shiloh? Once again, I didn't know then, I still don't know now. I don't know if rehashing through all of these notes and recordings has helped me find the clarity, the resolution that I thought that I needed.

What I do know is that unpacking all of these notes, letters and tapes has opened up thoughts, feelings, and dreams which I had boxed up years ago. I have no sustained regrets for immersing myself once again into this story, and I have found much satisfaction. I don't know where these energies will take me, but as sad as I am for the loss of Sarah, I am also ready to journey with God again.

EPILOGUE

That night, the pastor traveled again to the place he thought of as Heaven. That night, he found himself standing at the edge of a quiet lake. It was exactly the same spot where the woman stood at the end of his last dream of Heaven. That was her time and place, this is his. He was no longer an observer; he was singular, fully immersed where he now was. He was in Heaven, his earth-life ended.

He himself wasn't sure if he had died or not, whether this was a visit or forever, and he found that he didn't need to know. What he did know was that he was completely at ease. There was much which was familiar to him, and he was grateful for that. He found himself in the company of the same companions who guided the woman of his Heaven dreams. These companions still carry with them their quiet dignity and unselfish commitment and intent. It was now into his eyes that they spoke their sacred loyalty; it was now his soft skin which received their sandpapery scratch from their wild mane and hide.

So the pastor takes it all in. He finds himself in the middle of the familiar covering of Heaven's journey formation, lions around him, angels above him, and a wise, kindly woman behind him. There was calm, a quiet. Before him lay a vast, unlimited unknown and yet he felt as comfortable as one does when sitting on a front porch swing. He caught a whiff of deep pine forest and he wondered what he would see, what he would feel. He was fully alive and, even though he has seen this world before, he now fully knew its beauty and he smiled at the wonder of it all. There were tingles of joy reverberating within him; there was great beauty yet to be revealed.

    The pastor stared at the path put before him, and then they set off. As he walked he felt a beautiful melody awaken in his heart. He smiled. He wondered if there were lyrics to the beautiful melody. He smiled again. As he followed in the lion's stately strides, the pastor began to sing. "A wino needs his bottle, a hero needs his fall, and if the two get all mixed up, well you can chuck it all. They both need something special, a kiss upon the cheek, to keep them bouncing off the gutter, and headed for the street."

    The angels remained in their posture of noble detachment, but the lions roared in unison. They were pleased. The wise, serene woman softly chuckled, and off they went.

    The End.

CPSIA information can be obtained
at www.ICGtesting.com
Printed in the USA
BVHW031038190919
558892BV00002B/347/P